THE ATLAS OF
ENDANGERED SPECIES

Richard Mackay is a Senior Consultant at
ENVIRON, specialising in ecology. He has
undertaken wildlife surveys both in Britain and
further afield, including a report for the Aride
Island Nature Reserve, Seychelles. He has a wide
experience of environmental impact assessment,
as well as formulating environmental policies for
major companies.

In the same series:

 THE STATE OF THE WORLD ATLAS
by Dan Smith

 THE ATLAS OF WAR AND PEACE
by Dan Smith
with Ane Bræin

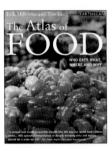 THE ATLAS OF FOOD
by Erik Millstone and Tim Lang

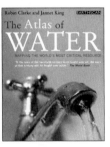 THE ATLAS OF WATER
by Robin Clarke and Jannet King

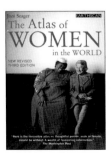 THE ATLAS OF WOMEN IN THE WORLD
by Joni Seager

THE ATLAS OF ENDANGERED SPECIES

Richard Mackay

London

First published by Earthscan in the UK in 2002
This revised edition first published in 2005

A catalogue record for this book is available from the British Library

ISBN: 1-84407-288-6

Produced for Earthscan by
Myriad Editions Limited
6–7 Old Steine, Brighton BN1 1EJ, UK
Tel: +44 (0)1273 606700
Fax: +44 (0)1273 606708
Email: info@MyriadEditions.com
Web: www.MyriadEditions.com

Edited and co-ordinated for Myriad Editions by
Candida Lacey and Jannet King
Design and graphics by Corinne Pearlman and Isabelle Lewis
Maps created by All Terrain Mapping and Isabelle Lewis
Additional research by Jannet King

Printed on paper produced from sustainable sources.
Printed and bound in Hong Kong through Phoenix Offset Limited
under the supervision of Bob Cassels, The Hanway Press, London

For a full list of publications please contact:

Earthscan
8–12 Camden High Street
London, NW1 0JH, UK
Tel: +44 (0)20 7387 8558
Fax: +44 (0)20 7387 8998
Email: earthinfo@earthscan.co.uk
Web: www.earthscan.co.uk

Earthscan is an imprint of James & James (Science Publishers) Ltd
and publishes in association with the International Institute for
Environment and Development

CONTENTS

IUCN Categories

The following categories are used throughout the book. For further details see:
   <www.redlist.org/info/categories_criteria.html>

Critically endangered – A taxon is critically endangered when it is facing an extremely high risk of extinction in the wild in the immediate future.

Endangered – A taxon is endangered when it is not critically endangered but is facing a very high risk of extinction in the wild in the near future.

Vulnerable – A taxon is vulnerable when it is not critically endangered or endangered but is facing a high risk of extinction in the wild in the medium-term future.

Evolutionary adaptation has given rise to a cornucopia of life. Of all the species that have ever lived, only a tiny fraction is alive today. Spasms in Earth's history, caused by volcanoes erupting and meteorites impacting, wiped out entire groups of organisms, and gradual climatic changes have eliminated others. The evolutionary strategies of some species were just not good enough and they succumbed to competitors and predators. The demise of the dinosaurs is a humbling tale. Their awesome size and power did not assure their survival. Quite the reverse: it left them slow to adapt to a changing environment and more vulnerable than mammals to catastrophic events.

As humans, the psychological trap of believing ourselves to be a class apart from other creatures is exacerbated by the absence of other living hominids. The Australopithecines, Homo ergaster and our other ancestors took tools, organization and culture well beyond the level of sophistication of the primates. Although we are of their line, the biological changes that accompanied their advancement are sufficient for us to consider ourselves a different "chrono-species".

Some parts of the world are more ecologically interesting than others. Habitats such as coral reefs and rainforests contain a great variety of species. Some intrigue us because, like the Arctic and Antarctic, their wildlife is peculiar and we have not yet heavily disturbed them. Species on islands such as Madagascar developed in geographical isolation, giving rise to unique forms. Australia has the dubious distinction of the most mammal extinctions. Many other regions and ecosystems are worthy of study but limited space precluded descriptions of them in this book.

A small fraction – probably fewer than ten percent – of living species have been identified and classified. The remaining 90 percent are mostly invertebrates. Consequently, an anomaly arises in that the most intensely researched countries show up as having the highest number of threatened species. The World Conservation Monitoring Centre, now a division of the United Nations Environment Programme, is the global data organization for conservation. IUCN-The World Conservation Union is the umbrella group for conservation bodies around the world. IUCN has promulgated a system for assessing whether a species is threatened and, if so, the severity of the risk. The definitive work is the organization's publication: the *IUCN Red List of Threatened Species.*

Representing the number of species threatened endorses the notion of a species as a closed gene-pool. This presents conceptual difficulties, such as in defining species among organisms that are "parthenogenetic" – they produce offspring from unfertilized eggs. Despite its flaws, however, the species concept is useful for conservation. Subspecies and isolated populations of species are not counted in this book, although they are sometimes described in the text.

The distribution of living things does not respect political boundaries. However, decisions affecting conservation are still usually made by states and their borders provide a convenient means of dividing the land surface. For groups of animals and plants, the level of threat has been represented in this atlas by the number of threatened species occurring in each country. This inevitably gives the impression that larger countries have greater conservation problems than smaller ones. To redress the balance, Part 6 "Issues of Conservation" highlights areas with the greatest biodiversity and those with the most endemic species.

Why should conserving biodiversity matter? Many people feel that we are stewards of the planet and that to annihilate species as we are doing is immoral. Quite apart from spiritual and aesthetic loss, each extinction also represents the loss of irreplaceable genetic information, including beneficial characteristics that could have been bred into domestic crops and livestock. Chemicals produced naturally are also used to develop pharmaceuticals. When "keystone" species become extinct the balance of whole ecosystems is threatened.

Global warming is one of a number of threats outlined in the *Millennium Ecosystem Assessment*, completed in March 2005. This was the first comprehensive global evaluation of the world's major ecosystems. The assessment found that 60 percent of ecosystem services (the benefits people obtain from ecosystems, such as fisheries and prevention of soil erosion) are being degraded or used unsustainably. Loss of species was identified as a major factor affecting both the resilience of natural services and less tangible spiritual or cultural values. The consequences for human well-being are severe, but by protecting ecosystem services in agriculture, industry and in our lifestyles, we can halt the decline.

Agreement between states can secure the conservation of common resources, such as ocean fisheries. It can also suppress damaging wildlife trade, driven by our fascination with the rare and exotic and the purported medicinal properties of some plants and animals. The Convention on International Trade in Endangered Species of Wild Fauna and Flora (CITES) was adopted in 1973. More recent treaties have addressed conservation within national jurisdictions. In 1992 the United Nations Conference on Environment and Development in Rio de Janeiro (the "Rio Summit") adopted the Convention on Biological Diversity, the Convention on Climate Change and Forest Principles. All are relevant to threatened species. Although the Convention on Biological Diversity restated the principle of national sovereignty, it also placed a duty on states to conserve biodiversity by requiring that environmental impact assessments be carried out for infrastructure projects, for example.

The size of the human population is of major consequence in conserving biodiversity. Fewer people would allow us to leave habitats intact or to exploit them sustainably. Of course the environmental impact, or "footprint", of individual countries differs. The USA, with four percent of the world's population, produces a quarter of the world's greenhouse-gas emissions. However, the USA and other industrialized countries also produce most of the world's clean technologies.

Pollution is a global issue. Carbon dioxide warms the whole planet, not just your back yard. The impact of global warming on threatened species will be profound. Polar bears will be stranded and starve as ice retreats. Plants with a limited distribution may not survive rising temperatures. Coasts and estuaries will be inundated. The world will lose species that have evolved over billions of years to form communities and habitats that without human interference would still exist in exquisite equilibrium.

The Convention on Climate Change went to the very heart of economic systems. An accord was signed in Kyoto in 1997, outlining binding limits on the global warming contributions of developed countries. The extent to which the transfer of clean technology to developing countries and "carbon sinks" could be debited from national emissions was contentious. In November 2000 talks in The Hague, Netherlands on the detail of the Kyoto agreement foundered on US intransigence but in July 2001 a compromise agreement was reached by 180 countries (excluding the USA). Following ratification by Russia, the Kyoto Protocol finally came into force on 16 February 2005. It is hoped that this represents a significant first step towards concerted international action on global warming.

My thanks go to Patricia Patton at WWF-UK, and to Alex Solyom at WWF-US, who kindly supplied most of the photographs included in this book, and to the photographers who have generously given us permission to use their images (see opposite for full photo credits).

I would also like to thank the Species Survival Commission of IUCN and Birdlife International, who were both helpful in clarifying data.

I am very grateful to the team at Myriad Editions – Jannet King, Candida Lacey and Corinne Pearlman – who worked tirelessly to ensure the rigour and visual impact of the book, and to the cartographers, Isabelle Lewis and Angela Wilson.

Another sincere acknowledgement is to my parents Judith and John, who gave their wholehearted support.

RICHARD MACKAY
London, May 2005

Richard Mackay and Myriad Editions are grateful to WWF in the USA and UK for permission to use a selection of images from the WWF photo archives. Known worldwide by its Panda logo, WWF is one of the largest and most accomplished international conservation organizations. With offices or resident representatives in more than 50 countries and field projects in more than 100 countries, WWF is working across the globe to protect endangered species and to save endangered spaces.

To learn more about WWF and its programs, visit the organization's portal website at <www.wwf.org>. WWF assumes no responsibility for the accuracy of the text, maps or charts in the atlas.

EXTINCTION IS FOREVER

1

"Pragmatic self-interest alone should teach us that
we must change before nature exacts inevitable revenge."

– David Watson,
author of *How Deep is Deep Ecology*

EVOLUTION

In 1831 the British naturalist Charles Darwin took a fateful voyage on the survey ship HMS *Beagle*. Over five years he studied the geology and wildlife of the lands the *Beagle* visited. He found fossils of species long extinct and wondered how new species had replaced them. His observations led him to deduce that the difference between species was an outcome of natural processes. Darwin's thesis culminated in the publication in 1859 of *On the Origin of Species*. Here he challenged the prevailing orthodoxy that the diversity of life was the product of supernatural design.

By Darwin's day the concept of a "species" was widely understood as a group of organisms that can breed with each other but cannot interbreed with another species. The Swedish botanist Karl von Linné (who became known by his Latin name of Carolus Linnaeus) had developed a system in the mid-18th century that classified organisms according to their similarities, placing them in a hierarchy that, at the highest level, makes the basic distinction between animals and plants. His approach forms the basis of modern-day taxonomic diagrams (see opposite).

The difference between the approach of Linnaeus and Darwin was that while Linnaeus saw his work as "mapping" the world God had created, Darwin was interested in explaining how living creatures evolved and continued to develop. Darwin observed that there is variation within a species and that some characteristics are more beneficial than others. He knew that the characteristics of an adult organism depend on its parents and the environment where it lives. As life is a competition for scarce resources and a test of resilience in the face of harsh conditions, organisms with characteristics most likely to allow them to survive will breed most successfully. Those characteristics will then become more prevalent within the species as it adapts – or evolves – to its changing circumstances. When events such as a rising sea level or the movement of the Earth's continents splits a population into two, the new populations cannot meet to interbreed. Over time, separate evolution will cause changes in each group to the point where they can no longer successfully reproduce with each other – a new species has evolved.

A taxonomic diagram, such as the simplified version opposite, relates species by their evolutionary history. Species of the same order are considered to share a more recent common ancestor than species of the same phylum. Different species with similar features are grouped into families. Similar families belong to an order, related orders to a class and classes to a phylum, each of which belongs to one of the kingdoms. There are, however, different criteria for assigning organisms to different groups, and continuing debates as how the divisions should be made, even at the highest level of the kingdom.

Darwin's theory of evolution is itself constantly being reviewed. In the 20th century scientists studying life at the molecular level recognized that natural selection occurs only indirectly between whole organisms (animals and plants). At a more fundamental level it is occurring between genes. This explains behaviors such as altruism: for example, ants will sacrifice themselves to defend their nests because what is important is the survival of the genes shared by related ants rather than survival of the individual.

EVOLUTION SIMPLIFIED
How a single species can evolve into many species

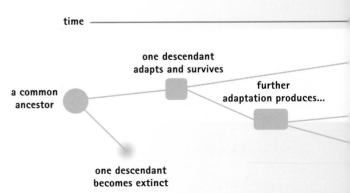

time

a common ancestor

one descendant adapts and survives

further adaptation produces...

one descendant becomes extinct

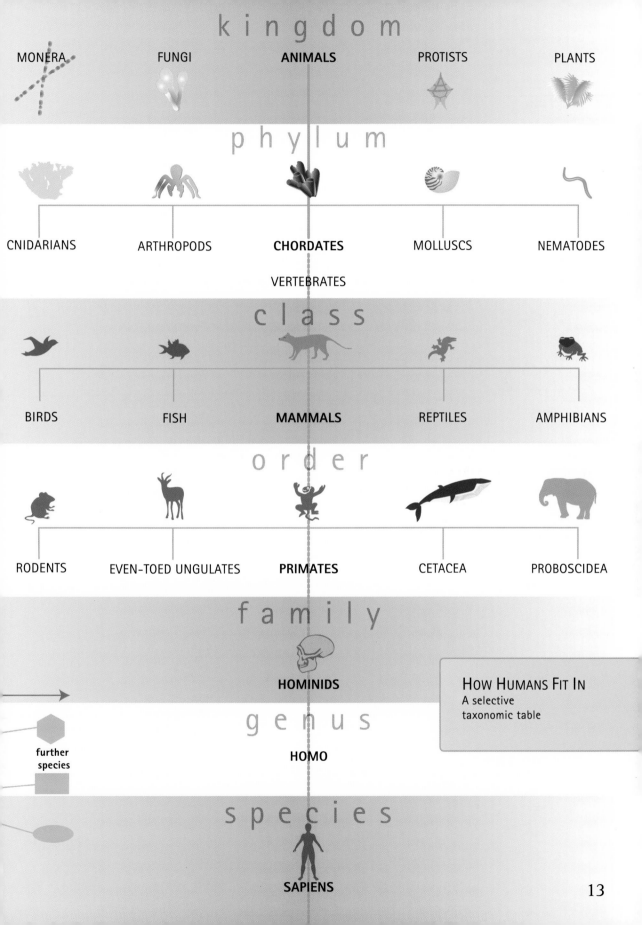

kingdom

MONERA · FUNGI · **ANIMALS** · PROTISTS · PLANTS

phylum

CNIDARIANS · ARTHROPODS · **CHORDATES** · MOLLUSCS · NEMATODES

VERTEBRATES

class

BIRDS · FISH · **MAMMALS** · REPTILES · AMPHIBIANS

order

RODENTS · EVEN-TOED UNGULATES · **PRIMATES** · CETACEA · PROBOSCIDEA

family

HOMINIDS

How Humans Fit In
A selective taxonomic table

genus

further species

HOMO

species

SAPIENS

13

MASS EXTINCTIONS

The "biodiversity" of a place or region is a measure of the number of species present and of their abundance. Each species occupies a "niche" – a specific location, relationship with its physical surroundings and mode of interaction with other species. Organisms of a single species in one place are called a population, and together populations form a community.

Species naturally become extinct as they fail to reproduce, either through extreme conditions or because of displacement by competitors. Even if a species adapts to these threats, it will, by definition, have evolved into a different species. Fossils suggest that this background rate of extinction is punctuated by short periods of mass extinction, defined as a period in which at least 50 percent of all species become extinct.

The precise cause of each mass extinction is difficult to assess. Catastrophes such as meteorite impacts and comet showers may have been responsible for some mass extinctions. Global climate change, fluctuation in the concentration of various gases, and other gradual environmental trends may have caused others.

Interactions between species could even have been a factor, creating instability in complex, finely balanced communities. The loss of certain "keystone" species can be particularly damaging to communities. For example, in areas where otters have recently been hunted nearly to extinction, sea urchins have multiplied, consuming the kelp and so radically altering the habitat. Keystone species may be as small as soil invertebrates or even microbes.

Mass extinctions overwhelmed creatures living both on land and in the sea. On land, animals seem to have suffered more than plants. In the sea, trilobites – a group of marine animals with hard shells – suffered a repeated loss of species.

Mass extinctions have occurred roughly every 26 million years. It is not clear if this pattern has arisen by chance, or whether there is some explanation for it. There have been five particularly widespread mass extinctions. The species that survived, subsequently diversified to occupy the niches vacated by those that vanished. Thus, new forms of life appeared.

The present age is witness to the sixth great

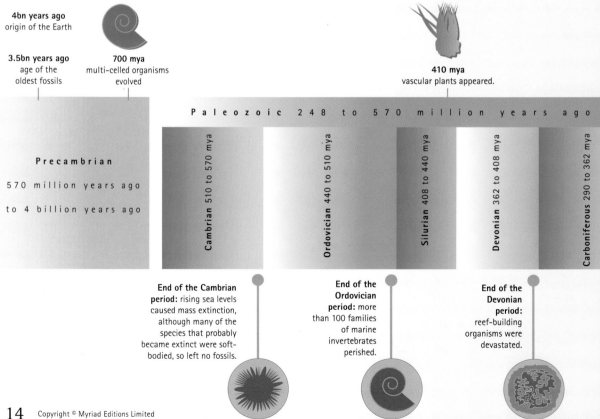

4bn years ago
origin of the Earth

3.5bn years ago
age of the oldest fossils

700 mya
multi-celled organisms evolved

410 mya
vascular plants appeared.

Paleozoic 248 to 570 million years ago

Precambrian

570 million years ago

to 4 billion years ago

Cambrian 510 to 570 mya

Ordovician 440 to 510 mya

Silurian 408 to 440 mya

Devonian 362 to 408 mya

Carboniferous 290 to 362 mya

End of the Cambrian period: rising sea levels caused mass extinction, although many of the species that probably became extinct were soft-bodied, so left no fossils.

End of the Ordovician period: more than 100 families of marine invertebrates perished.

End of the Devonian period: reef-building organisms were devastated.

mass extinction. Although 1.5 million living species have been named by scientists, this is but a small fraction of the estimated 10 million to 100 million species that are thought to be alive on Earth. Most of these are likely to be destroyed by humans before they have even been identified.

240 mya
dinosaurs, mammals, pterosaurs (flying reptiles), amphibians (including frogs and turtles) appeared.

100,000 years ago
homo sapiens appeared

210 mya
towards the end of the Triassic period, climate change caused an extinction of amphibians, marine reptiles and other species, setting the stage for the ascendance of dinosaurs.

190 mya
birds appeared

130 mya
flowering plants (angiosperms) appeared

50 mya
primates evolved

11,000 years ago
a cooling climate and hunting by humans caused extinctions among large mammals, including mammoths, huge ground sloths and saber-toothed tigers.

M e s o z o i c 6 5   t o   2 4 8   m i l l i o n   y e a r s   a g o   **C e n z o i c** 0 to 65 mya

Permian 248 to 290 mya

Triassic 206 to 248 mya

Jurassic 145 to 206 mya

Cretaceous 65 to 145 mya

Tertiary 2 to 65 mya

Quatenary 0 to 2 mya

End of the Permian period: between 90% and 95% of marine species disappeared, including trilobites.

End of the Cretaceous period: 85% of all species, including the dinosaurs, became extinct. The presence of iridium in 66-million-year-old rocks suggests that a meteorite strike shrouded the planet in dust and darkness. Alternatively, the extinction could have been caused by gradual climate change.

Present: In the 20th century the rate of extinction increased to 1% each year – about 10,000 times higher than before human technological society.

15

HOMINIDS

Modern humans are the last survivors of the hominid family whose many branches evolved as a result of geographic isolation, possibly brought about by climate change.

Humans are the only primates who habitually stand and move in an upright position. The oldest known hominids are the genus *Australopithecus*, which evolved from more ape-like creatures over 4 million years ago in Africa and appears not to have spread beyond that continent. Their jaws were ideally suited to feeding on fruit, nuts and berries, and they became extinct around one million years ago probably because their specialized diet became scarce as the climate became drier and savannah replaced woodland.

By the time of its demise, *Australopithecus* was not the only hominid in existence. Two and a half million years ago a larger-brained hominid developed, and evolved into a species (*Homo sapiens*) that was to dominate the planet.

Hominid skulls increased in size as the species evolved, indicating a growing mental capacity. From the size and form of different brain areas, scientists have been able to deduce how intelligence has developed: the frontal lobe indicates abstract processing and a capacity for language whilst the parietal lobe, at the top of the head, is responsible for technological and computational thinking.

It is this use of tools and technology, from clothing and housing to sophisticated farming methods, that has served as a buffer between *Homo sapiens* and the changing environment. Alterations in the population gene pool that lead eventually to new species developing have not been identified in humans for the last 250,000 years.

About two and a half million years ago hominids began fashioning bladed tools by chipping rocks. The same ability for technological and computational thinking now presents opportunities for genetic manipulation and artificial body-parts – a development that may lead to the most rapid, awesome and potentially terrifying period of hominid evolution yet witnessed.

Homo neanderthalensis lived in Southern Europe 100,000 years ago. Up until about 30,000 years ago, they co-existed with modern humans. Their demise may have been due to competition for resources with humans or it is possible they met a more violent end. Alternative theories suggest that Neanderthals were adapted to cold conditions and disappeared as the climate grew warmer. Although some scientists argue that Neanderthals gave rise to modern humans, most agree that they are not our direct ancestors.

Hominids are human-like primates, descended from the genus **Homo**. Bones of *Homo erectus* have been discovered across South and Southeast Asia. They became extinct about 150,000 years ago – before the appearance of *Homo sapiens* around 120,000 years ago.

FOSSIL FINDS IN AFRICA

- area where fossils have been found
- **A** Australopithecus
- **H** Homo

H erectus

H erectus

A bahrelghazali

A afarensis

A anamensis
A afarensis
A boisei
H erectus
H habilis
H rudolfensis

A africanus
A robustus
H habilis

Most fossil finds are just fragments, such as a tooth or a piece of skull. **"Lucy"** is special because almost half of her skeleton was recovered and DNA testing showed that she lived 3.2 million years ago.

Lucy was discovered in the Hatar Valley in Ethiopia by Donald Johanson in 1974, and named after the Beatles' song, "Lucy in the Sky with Diamonds" (remade by Elton John that year). Lucy was probably around 25 years old when she died. She would have stood about 3 feet 6 inches (1.10 meters) tall, although other *Australopithecus afarensis* from this area were up to 5 feet 8 inches (1.70 meters) tall.

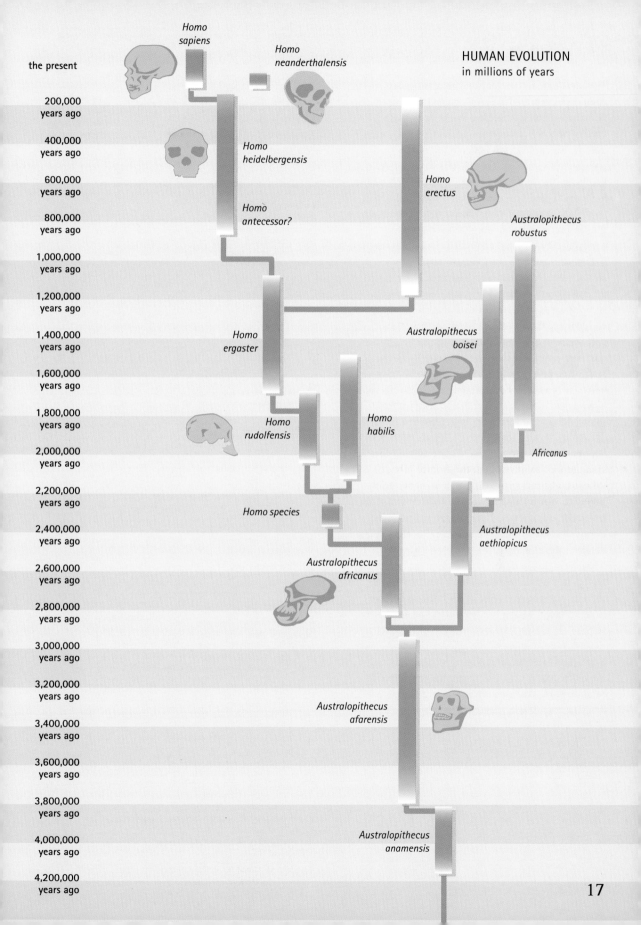

HUMAN EVOLUTION
in millions of years

the present

200,000 years ago

400,000 years ago

600,000 years ago

800,000 years ago

1,000,000 years ago

1,200,000 years ago

1,400,000 years ago

1,600,000 years ago

1,800,000 years ago

2,000,000 years ago

2,200,000 years ago

2,400,000 years ago

2,600,000 years ago

2,800,000 years ago

3,000,000 years ago

3,200,000 years ago

3,400,000 years ago

3,600,000 years ago

3,800,000 years ago

4,000,000 years ago

4,200,000 years ago

Homo sapiens

Homo neanderthalensis

Homo heidelbergensis

Homo antecessor?

Homo erectus

Australopithecus robustus

Homo ergaster

Australopithecus boisei

Homo rudolfensis

Homo habilis

Africanus

Homo species

Australopithecus aethiopicus

Australopithecus africanus

Australopithecus afarensis

Australopithecus anamensis

17

HUMAN ENVIRONMENTAL IMPACT

The total human demand on the planet's natural resources exceeds the Earth's capacity by 20 percent. Since emerging as the dominant species of the *Homo* genus, around 30,000 years ago, *Homo sapiens* has become the most powerful, creative, and ultimately destructive, life-form on the planet. The rate at which humans have multiplied and congregated into vast urban sprawls makes such demands on the environment that in places it is cracking under the strain.

Mining, the burning of fossil fuels and other polluting industrial activities, intensive agriculture involving excessive chemicals, deforestation for timber and agriculture, the creation of road networks that fragment ecosystems, the paving of the Earth's surface, and the over extraction of water from aquifers – all these activities are changing the environment irrevocably. The delicate balance between the species that make up the Earth's rich and varied ecosystems has been disrupted, and thousands of life forms are being pushed towards extinction by the activities of a single species.

By destroying ecosystems, we are sewing the seeds of our own destruction, because it is on these very ecosystems that we depend for our survival. Forests absorb carbon dioxide and stop soil from being washed away, mangroves filter impurities and protect the coastline, oceans help regulate the climate.

Signs of global warming are apparent across the world. It is occurring at such a rate that few of the Earth's species – least of all humans – have time to adapt. Rising temperatures and more unpredictable weather patterns are leading to floods and droughts. Sea levels are rising. Animal migratory patterns, and plant growing seasons are changing, often upsetting mutually dependent relationships. Diseases are extending in range. And the way of life – indeed the very survival – of millions of people and hundreds of thousands of other species, is threatened.

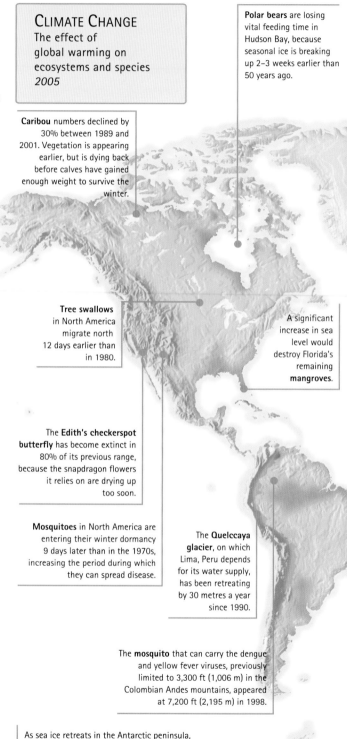

CLIMATE CHANGE
The effect of global warming on ecosystems and species
2005

Polar bears are losing vital feeding time in Hudson Bay, because seasonal ice is breaking up 2–3 weeks earlier than 50 years ago.

Caribou numbers declined by 30% between 1989 and 2001. Vegetation is appearing earlier, but is dying back before calves have gained enough weight to survive the winter.

Tree swallows in North America migrate north 12 days earlier than in 1980.

A significant increase in sea level would destroy Florida's remaining **mangroves**.

The **Edith's checkerspot butterfly** has become extinct in 80% of its previous range, because the snapdragon flowers it relies on are drying up too soon.

Mosquitoes in North America are entering their winter dormancy 9 days later than in the 1970s, increasing the period during which they can spread disease.

The **Quelccaya glacier**, on which Lima, Peru depends for its water supply, has been retreating by 30 metres a year since 1990.

The **mosquito** that can carry the dengue and yellow fever viruses, previously limited to 3,300 ft (1,006 m) in the Colombian Andes mountains, appeared at 7,200 ft (2,195 m) in 1998.

As sea ice retreats in the Antarctic peninsula, **Adelie penguins** are declining, and being replaced by gentoo penguins moving south from more temperate regions.

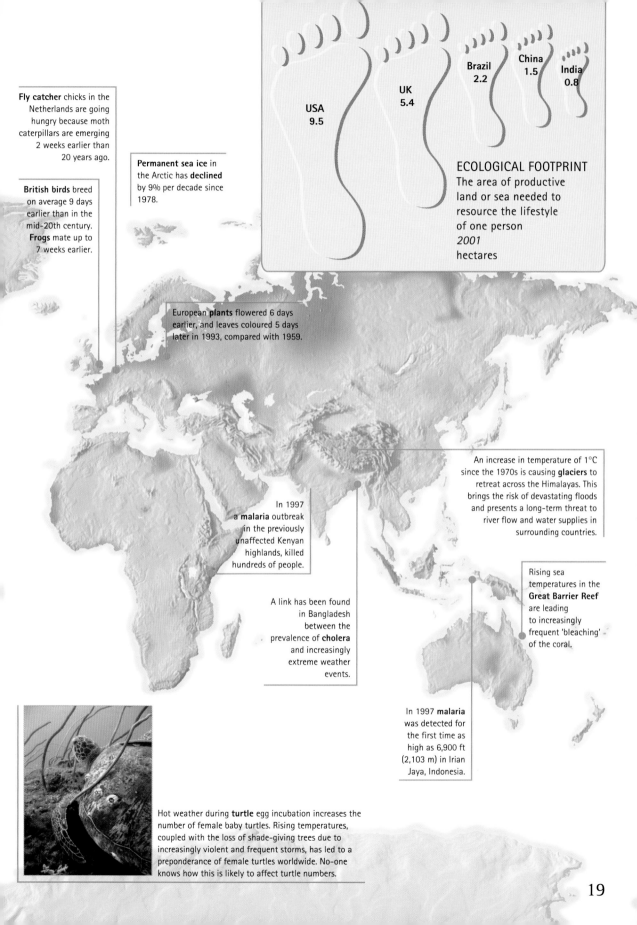

ECOLOGICAL FOOTPRINT
The area of productive land or sea needed to resource the lifestyle of one person
2001
hectares

USA 9.5
UK 5.4
Brazil 2.2
China 1.5
India 0.8

Fly catcher chicks in the Netherlands are going hungry because moth caterpillars are emerging 2 weeks earlier than 20 years ago.

British birds breed on average 9 days earlier than in the mid-20th century. **Frogs** mate up to 7 weeks earlier.

Permanent sea ice in the Arctic has **declined** by 9% per decade since 1978.

European **plants** flowered 6 days earlier, and leaves coloured 5 days later in 1993, compared with 1959.

An increase in temperature of 1°C since the 1970s is causing **glaciers** to retreat across the Himalayas. This brings the risk of devastating floods and presents a long-term threat to river flow and water supplies in surrounding countries.

In 1997 a **malaria** outbreak in the previously unaffected Kenyan highlands, killed hundreds of people.

Rising sea temperatures in the **Great Barrier Reef** are leading to increasingly frequent 'bleaching' of the coral.

A link has been found in Bangladesh between the prevalence of **cholera** and increasingly extreme weather events.

In 1997 **malaria** was detected for the first time as high as 6,900 ft (2,103 m) in Irian Jaya, Indonesia.

Hot weather during **turtle** egg incubation increases the number of female baby turtles. Rising temperatures, coupled with the loss of shade-giving trees due to increasingly violent and frequent storms, has led to a preponderance of female turtles worldwide. No-one knows how this is likely to affect turtle numbers.

19

ECOSYSTEMS

"Try to imagine the Earth without ecosystems...
Each ecosystem represents a solution to a particular
challenge to life, worked out over millennia...
Stripped of its ecosystems, Earth would resemble
the stark, lifeless images beamed back from Mars..."

— *World Resources 2000–2001*

TROPICAL FORESTS

The area bounded by the Tropic of Cancer (23.5°N) and the Tropic of Capricorn (23.5°S) is known as "the tropics". Tropical rainforest, mainly comprised of evergreen trees, thrives in areas of high rainfall. Deciduous trees, which shed their leaves in the dry season, tend to grow in areas where there is a seasonal drought. In dry areas that are prone to fire, and where soils are particularly poor, trees grow sparsely, forming "woody savanna".

Tropical forests bind the soil, helping to prevent erosion and retain the few nutrients present. They also absorb carbon dioxide from the atmosphere, exchanging it for oxygen. Tropical forests cover only 6 percent of the Earth's land area but probably contain over half the world's species, most of which have yet to be identified.

Fire, often caused by lightning, is part of the natural cycle of regeneration in tropical forests. Fire destroys the forest canopy, enabling light to reach the ground, and saplings and herbs to grow. In most cases, however, forest fires are caused by humans. In some cases they are deliberately lit in order to clear forests for agriculture. In others, they are started inadvertently, perhaps by discarded cigarettes or sparks from machinery.

Clearing by slashing and burning techniques, and more recently by machines, may completely destroy the remaining major areas of tropical forests. Many of the tropical forests are in poor countries whose priorities are to clear land for agriculture. Attempts by wealthier countries to encourage development often lead to tropical forests being exploited for timber.

Once the forest is gone, the land is prone to erosion and flooding. Nutrients in the soil are rapidly leached and after a few years farming and ranching become untenable. Where the original forest cover is substantial, as in the Amazon, it has a major influence on climate. Loss of trees reduces local rainfall and may even disrupt the global climate. Sustainable exploitation of tropical forests, including selective logging and harvesting of products such as fruit and rubber, can provide a higher long-term income than more destructive practices.

PROTECTED TROPICAL FOREST
Percentage of tropical forest protected *1996*

- 50% or more
- 30.0% – 49.9%
- 10.0% – 29.9%
- 5.0% – 9.9%
- 0.1% – 4.9%
- 0% or no data
- no tropical forest

The **mahogany tree** is prized worldwide for its dark timber, and about 40% of mahogany logged in Brazil is exported to make furniture. The trees grow slowly, at low density, and the mahogany is already extinct in Honduras and Colombia.

UNITED STATES OF AMERICA

MEXICO

CUBA

DOMINICAN REPUBLIC

BELIZE JAMAICA HAITI
GUATEMALA HONDURAS
EL SALVADOR NICARAGUA

COSTA RICA

PANAMA

TRINIDAD & TOBAGO

VENEZUELA GUYANA
SURINAME

COLOMBIA

ECUADOR

SENEGAL
GAMBIA
GUINEA-BISSAU
GUINEA
SIERRA LEONE
LIBERIA

BRAZIL

PERU

BOLIVIA

PARAGUAY

ARGENTINA

TROPICAL FOREST BY REGION
Protected tropical forest as percentage of tropical forest in the region *1996*

- tropical forest area in thousand hectares
- percentage protected

Asia
16.4%

210,720

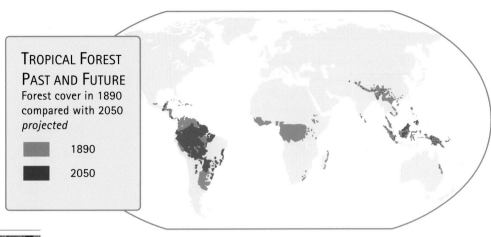

TROPICAL FOREST PAST AND FUTURE
Forest cover in 1890 compared with 2050 *projected*

- 1890
- 2050

Tropical forests in the **Congo basin** are being degraded at a rate that may see them disappear by 2050, as rapid population growth and a desperate need to repay international debt drives indiscriminate logging.

EGYPT

MALI
NIGER
CHAD
SUDAN
ERITREA
BURKINA FASO
NIGERIA
BENIN
CENTRAL AFRICAN REPUBLIC
ETHIOPIA
GHANA
TOGO
CÔTE d'IVOIRE
CAMEROON
EQUATORIAL GUINEA
UGANDA
SOMALIA
GABON
DEMOCRATIC REPUBLIC OF CONGO
KENYA
CONGO
RWANDA
BURUNDI
TANZANIA
ANGOLA
MALAWI
ZAMBIA
MADAGASCAR
ZIMBABWE
MOZAMBIQUE
NAMIBIA
BOTSWANA
SOUTH AFRICA
LESOTHO

CHINA
PAKISTAN
NEPAL
BHUTAN
INDIA
BANGLADESH
BURMA
LAOS
VIETNAM
THAILAND
CAMBODIA
SRI LANKA
PHILIPPINES
MALAYSIA
INDONESIA
PAPUA NEW GUINEA
AUSTRALIA

○ SOLOMON ISLANDS
◎ FIJI

In Indonesia vast areas of forest have been cleared for plantations of exotic species of tree, mainly to supply the market for wood pulp. Fires are used to clear native forest, but often run out of control.

Sub-Saharan Africa
9.1%

Central America and Caribbean
12%

South America
12.2%

Oceania
9.1%

448,063

70,812

620,514

53,560

23

TEMPERATE FORESTS

Temperate regions lie to the north and south of the tropics (23.5° latitude). Deciduous temperate trees shed their leaves each winter. Nearer the poles "boreal" forests of conifers cover the largest area of any forest type in the world. Conifers also dominate temperate forests at higher altitudes and in places where soils are poor.

Temperate forests have been cleared for agriculture and felled for timber for thousands of years. In the late 20th century this trend slowed as populations in temperate regions stabilized and resources other than timber were used for fuel and building materials. In the 1990s the area of temperate forest cover worldwide rose. However, the ecological quality of many forests has continued to decline as plantations replaced "old growth" forests and the frequency of fires has risen. Fires started by people consume an average of one percent of the existing Mediterranean forest every year.

Inappropriate planting of trees to act as "carbon sinks", a measure to counteract global warming, can actually reduce biodiversity. Most plantations are comprised of a few or even a single tree species such as eucalyptus and pine that may be alien to that habitat. Plantations do, however, make an indirect contribution to conservation by relieving the need to log "old growth" forests.

When forests become fragmented the plants and animals in each forest fragment can be isolated from adjacent forests and local extinction may result. It also becomes more difficult for species to migrate in response to climate change.

Pollution has also damaged temperate forests. The burning of fossil fuels releases sulfur and nitrogen into the atmosphere. Transported by the wind this can fall to earth as dry deposits or combine with water to form "acid rain". Polluting gases are also converted by sunlight into ozone, which interferes with the biological functioning of plants. Forests hundreds of miles from industrial centers are affected, in particular those in the northeast of North America, in East Asia and in northeastern Europe and Scandinavia.

TEMPERATE FOREST BY REGION

Protected temperate forest as percentage of temperate forest in the region *1996*

- temperate forest area in thousand hectares
- percentage protected

Asia
5.3%
132,065

North America
8.9%
683,700

South America
15.8%
39,178

Europe
3%
991,346

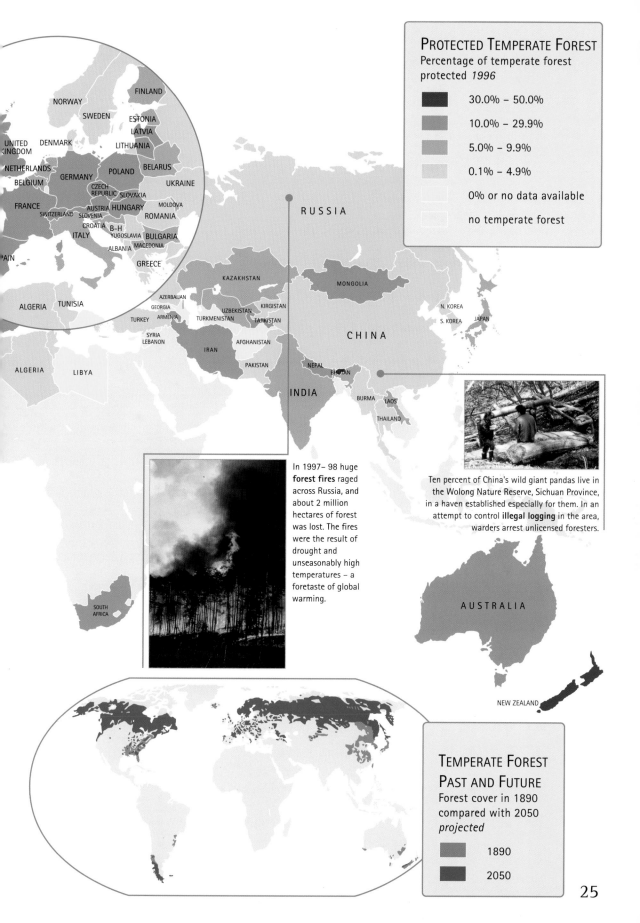

PROTECTED TEMPERATE FOREST
Percentage of temperate forest protected *1996*

- 30.0% – 50.0%
- 10.0% – 29.9%
- 5.0% – 9.9%
- 0.1% – 4.9%
- 0% or no data available
- no temperate forest

Map labels (Europe inset):
NORWAY, FINLAND, SWEDEN, ESTONIA, LATVIA, LITHUANIA, UNITED KINGDOM, DENMARK, NETHERLANDS, BELARUS, POLAND, BELGIUM, GERMANY, CZECH REPUBLIC, SLOVAKIA, UKRAINE, FRANCE, SWITZERLAND, AUSTRIA, HUNGARY, SLOVENIA, MOLDOVA, ROMANIA, ITALY, CROATIA, B-H, YUGOSLAVIA, BULGARIA, ALBANIA, MACEDONIA, GREECE, SPAIN

**Map labels (main):**
RUSSIA, KAZAKHSTAN, MONGOLIA, N. KOREA, S. KOREA, JAPAN, AZERBAIJAN, GEORGIA, ARMENIA, TURKEY, UZBEKISTAN, KIRGISTAN, TAJIKISTAN, TURKMENISTAN, CHINA, SYRIA, LEBANON, IRAN, AFGHANISTAN, ALGERIA, TUNISIA, ALGERIA, LIBYA, PAKISTAN, NEPAL, BHUTAN, INDIA, BURMA, LAOS, THAILAND, SOUTH AFRICA, AUSTRALIA, NEW ZEALAND

In 1997– 98 huge **forest fires** raged across Russia, and about 2 million hectares of forest was lost. The fires were the result of drought and unseasonably high temperatures – a foretaste of global warming.

Ten percent of China's wild giant pandas live in the Wolong Nature Reserve, Sichuan Province, in a haven established especially for them. In an attempt to control **illegal logging** in the area, warders arrest unlicensed foresters.

TEMPERATE FOREST PAST AND FUTURE
Forest cover in 1890 compared with 2050 *projected*

- 1890
- 2050

25

GRASSLANDS

Grassland covers more of the Earth's surface than any other type of terrain. Estimates range from 31 percent to 43 percent, depending on the definition of "grassland", which can include savanna, prairie, scrub, high-altitude plains and Arctic tundra. More than 70 percent of some African countries are covered in grassland, and grassland makes up more than half the terrain in around 40 countries. One of the defining characteristics of grassland is that its vegetation is prevented from turning into forest by fire, grazing, lack of water or by freezing temperatures.

Grasslands support a wide range of wild animals, in particular birds. As well as providing year-round habitat for endemic bird species, grasslands also provide temporary refuge and breeding sites for migrating birds. They are therefore of vital importance, and their degradation in North America has resulted in a declining bird population since the mid-1960s.

Grasslands also provide grazing for domestic animals. In some areas of the world they have supported nomadic herds of sheep, goats and cattle for thousands of years. With growing human populations rearing ever more livestock, however, grasslands are at risk from over-grazing, which leads to soil erosion.

One of the major threats to grassland ecosystems is fragmentation by development, including roads. Breaking grassland up into small patches reduces its capacity to maintain biological diversity — it becomes degraded. This is what is happening in the Great Plains of the USA, where criss-crossing roads have fragmented 70 percent of the area into patches smaller than 386 square miles (1,000 square kilometres).

Much of the watershed areas of many of the world's largest rivers are comprised of grassland. Here it performs the vital function of absorbing rainfall into underground aquifers that in turn feed into the river systems. Grasslands also absorb carbon emissions, holding an estimated 33 percent of carbon stored in terrestrial ecosystems, most of which is to be found in the soil.

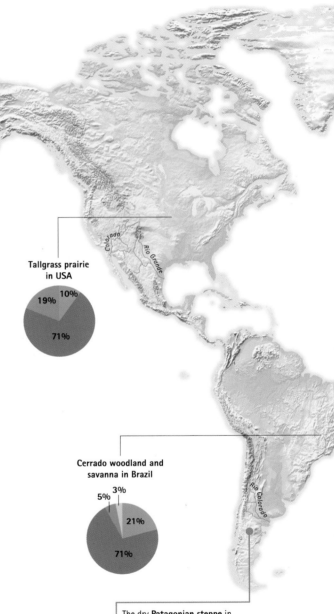

Tallgrass prairie in USA

10%
19%
71%

Cerrado woodland and savanna in Brazil

3%
5%
21%
71%

The dry **Patagonian steppe** in Argentina hosts abundant wildlife, including the endemic wild llama, the "guanaco". Human settlement is limited to "estancias" (ranches) and a few small towns. Its aridity leaves the Patagonian steppe vulnerable to overgrazing by sheep and goats, which are turning some areas into desert. Pumas are hunted, often illegally, because they prey on livestock.

The grassland of **Asia's high steppes** supports around 30 million livestock, many of which are grazed on a nomadic system. However, over the past 50 years Russian and Chinese herders have been encouraged to adopt more sedentary grazing methods mixed with arable farming. As a result, the fragile ecology of their grassland has been unbalanced, and around 75% has been degraded. Although the grassland in Mongolia is in better condition it is also now threatened by an increase in livestock grazed as a result of privatization since 1990.

Asian steppes

2%
6%
20%
72%

Woody savanna in central southern Africa

0.4%
7.6%
19%
73%

Once common across the Indian subcontinent, the **great Indian bustard** is now on the verge of extinction because livestock overgraze its grassland habitat.

Southwest Australian shrublands and woodlands

2% 4%
37%
57%

GRASSLANDS
Major areas of grassland
2000

☐ grassland

Current land use as percentage of estimated total grassland zone in selected areas

— remaining grassland
— converted to cropland
— converted to urban areas
— other

27

WETLANDS

Wetlands are among the world's richest and most productive ecosystems. They include swamps, marshes, mangroves, lakes and rivers and cover over 2 million square miles (5.7 million sq km).

Wetlands occur on poorly drained land, where organic matter decays very slowly and peat accumulates, creating bogs. At northern latitudes mosses such as *Sphagnum* dominate the flora. Where the soil has more nutrients, both inland and at the mouths of great rivers such as the Mississippi and the Nile, grass grows to form marshes. Mangroves, adapted to live in muddy tidal water that alternates between salty seawater and fresh, occur around deltas and elsewhere. They are mainly found in the tropics, but where ocean currents are favorable, occur also on sub-tropical coasts.

Salt marshes support a large number of invertebrates, which are preyed upon by diverse species of birds. Mangrove forests support lichens, orchids, and bacteria, and provide nesting sites for birds, and vital nursery and feeding sites for fish, crustaceans and other shellfish.

Agriculture is the principal cause of wetland destruction, but the damming of rivers can also disrupt these delicate ecosystems. Many wetlands have also been drained in an attempt to destroy the breeding sites of mosquitoes, and thereby control malaria. Wetlands have already been lost in Europe and North America and losses are now high in Asia and Africa. Inter-tidal salt marshes have been "reclaimed" and mangroves destroyed for the development of ports, marinas, housing and commercial fisheries. But salt marshes and mangroves provide vital ecological functions, helping to stabilize estuary banks and provide a barrier against the sea. Their destruction causes erosion and land subsidence and permits salt water to penetrate coastal soils and threaten fresh water supplies.

The Convention on Wetlands was signed in Ramsar, Iran in 1971. By 2005, 1,429 sites were included in the Ramsar List of Wetlands of International Importance. This represented over 125 million hectares wetlands, 50 percent more than in 2001. Signatories to the Convention undertake to practise "wise use" of those wetlands, to sustain their biodiversity.

FLORIDA MANGROVES

■ mangroves

— boundary of National Park

Tampa

F l o r i d a

Lake Worth

Miami

Everglades National Park World Heritage Site

Biscayne Bay National Park

Florida Keys

Florida has an estimated 765 square miles (2,000 sq km) of mangrove forests, comprising three different species: the red, black and white mangrove. During the 20th century large swathes were destroyed as the area was developed, including 44% in Tampa Bay, and 87% of those around Lake Worth. Even the conservation measures adopted in the Everglades National Park are not enough to protect it from water pollution. Florida's wading birds, which depend on mangroves for their nesting areas, have declined to around 10% of their original level.

CANADA

UNITED STATES OF AMERICA

MEXICO

CUBA

BAHAMAS

JAMAICA

DOMINICAN REP.

BELIZE

GUATEMALA   HONDURAS

EL SALVADOR   NICARAGUA

COSTA RICA

PANAMA

ST LUCIA

TRINIDAD & TOBAGO

VENEZUELA

SURINAME

COLOMBIA

ECUADOR

PERU

BRAZIL

BOLIVIA

PARAGUAY

CHILE

URUGUAY

ARGENTINA

MAURITANIA

SENEGAL

GAMBIA

GUINEA-BISSAU

GUINEA

SIERRA LEONE

The total annual value of ecosystem services provided by tidal marshes and mangroves worldwide is estimated at US$1.6 trillion.

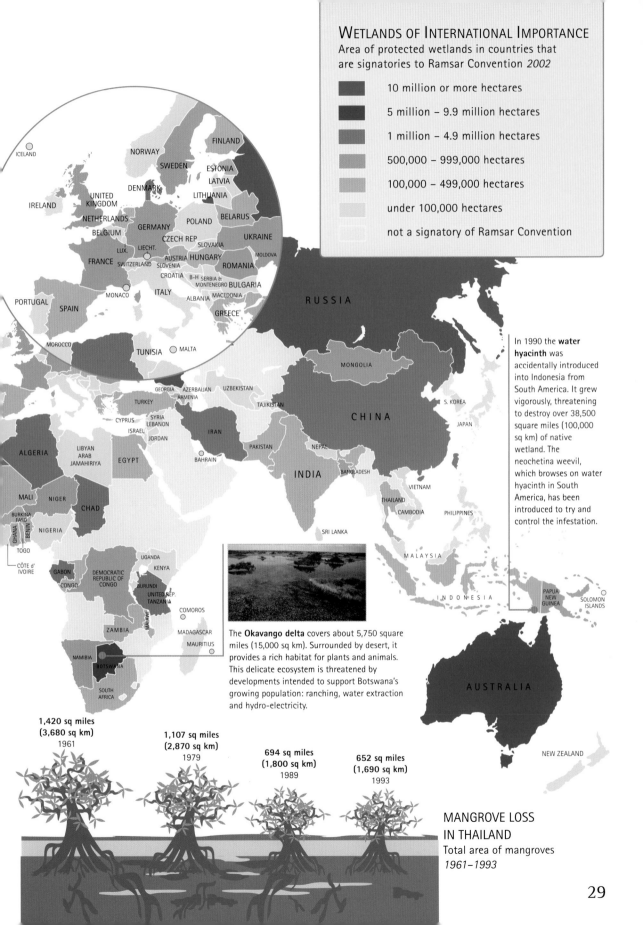

WETLANDS OF INTERNATIONAL IMPORTANCE
Area of protected wetlands in countries that
are signatories to Ramsar Convention *2002*

- 10 million or more hectares
- 5 million – 9.9 million hectares
- 1 million – 4.9 million hectares
- 500,000 – 999,000 hectares
- 100,000 – 499,000 hectares
- under 100,000 hectares
- not a signatory of Ramsar Convention

ICELAND
NORWAY FINLAND
SWEDEN ESTONIA
DENMARK LATVIA
LITHUANIA
UNITED KINGDOM
IRELAND BELARUS
NETHERLANDS GERMANY POLAND
BELGIUM UKRAINE
LUX. CZECH REP
LIECHT. SLOVAKIA
FRANCE SWITZERLAND AUSTRIA HUNGARY MOLDOVA
SLOVENIA ROMANIA
CROATIA B-H SERBIA & BULGARIA
MONACO SERBIA & MONTENEGRO
PORTUGAL SPAIN ITALY ALBANIA MACEDONIA
GREECE
MOROCCO
TUNISIA MALTA

RUSSIA

MONGOLIA

GEORGIA AZERBAIJAN UZBEKISTAN
ARMENIA
TURKEY TAJIKISTAN
CYPRUS SYRIA S. KOREA
LEBANON
ISRAEL JORDAN IRAN CHINA JAPAN
ALGERIA LIBYAN ARAB JAMAHIRIYA EGYPT BAHRAIN PAKISTAN NEPAL
INDIA BANGLADESH
MALI NIGER VIETNAM
CHAD THAILAND
BURKINA FASO CAMBODIA PHILIPPINES
GHANA NIGERIA SRI LANKA
BENIN
TOGO
CÔTE d'IVOIRE
GABON UGANDA MALAYSIA
CONGO KENYA
DEMOCRATIC REPUBLIC OF CONGO BURUNDI
UNITED REP. TANZANIA
MALAWI COMOROS
ZAMBIA MADAGASCAR
MAURITIUS INDONESIA PAPUA NEW GUINEA SOLOMON ISLANDS
NAMIBIA
BOTSWANA
SOUTH AFRICA AUSTRALIA

NEW ZEALAND

In 1990 the **water hyacinth** was accidentally introduced into Indonesia from South America. It grew vigorously, threatening to destroy over 38,500 square miles (100,000 sq km) of native wetland. The neochetina weevil, which browses on water hyacinth in South America, has been introduced to try and control the infestation.

The **Okavango delta** covers about 5,750 square miles (15,000 sq km). Surrounded by desert, it provides a rich habitat for plants and animals. This delicate ecosystem is threatened by developments intended to support Botswana's growing population: ranching, water extraction and hydro-electricity.

1,420 sq miles
(3,680 sq km)
1961

1,107 sq miles
(2,870 sq km)
1979

694 sq miles
(1,800 sq km)
1989

652 sq miles
(1,690 sq km)
1993

MANGROVE LOSS
IN THAILAND
Total area of mangroves
1961–1993

29

CORAL REEFS

Coral consists of thousands of invertebrate marine animals – known as "polyps" – with a hollow, cylindrical structure and a skeleton containing calcium carbonate. The lower end of the coral is attached to a rock or another polyp. At the free end is a mouth, surrounded by tentacles that can be extended to paralyze prey.

Coral reefs form in shallow ocean areas. Initial polyps divide into daughter polyps, which in turn divide to form colonies that can grow up to several yards wide. Corals are found in the waters of over 100 countries. They grow profusely in warm, well-circulating calm waters and cover an estimated 231,600 square miles (600,000 sq km) worldwide. Home to a vast number of different species, coral reefs are second only to rainforests in species richness.

Sick coral provides an early warning that entire ecosystems are in danger. Since the 1980s, dozens of new infections, including white band and yellow pox, have attacked corals. Few of these ailments have a known cause, but human development of coastal zones is a likely factor.

Increases in sea temperature and levels, and alterations to ocean currents, can cause individual polyps to "bleach". With increasing climate change, corals may not fully recover.

Forest clearance and intensive agriculture can wash soil into rivers and out to sea, silting up reefs. Sunlight is vital for coral growth but murky water prevents it reaching the reefs. The mangroves that protect reefs from terrestrial sediments are themselves under threat. When poorly treated sewage and fertilizer run-off flows over reefs, algae multiply in the nutrient-rich water, cover and choke the coral polyps.

Illegal fishing methods, such as the use of cyanide and explosives to stun fish, damages coral. Over-fishing also affects the ecological balance of a reef, which can become overgrown with algae if grazing fish are removed.

The loss of coral reefs is likely to reduce the fish catch of many tropical developing countries, around 25 percent of which comes from reef environments. Where reefs may have acted as barriers against erosion, their destruction may also allow the sea to encroach on coastal regions.

2% — pre-1998

ARABIAN REGION

33% in 1998

6% critical

6% future critical

CAPE VERDE

Arabian Sea

MALDIVES

In 1988, the severe "El Niño" phenomenon – when the ocean-atmosphere system in the tropical Pacific is disrupted and affects weather conditions worldwide – coupled with global warming, caused massive coral bleaching. Reefs in the northern Indian Ocean were particularly badly damaged.

Indian Ocean

13% pre-1998

46% in 1998

INDIAN OCEAN

12% critical

11% future critical

Two-thirds of all damage to coral in the Red Sea is caused by tourism, with tourists buying or taking coral, and inexperienced divers colliding with reefs. Carefully managed tourism could save reefs by developing the marine parks which act as breeding grounds for fish. However, although over 350 protected areas include coral reefs, these are often in countries without adequate resources to enforce the necessary controls.

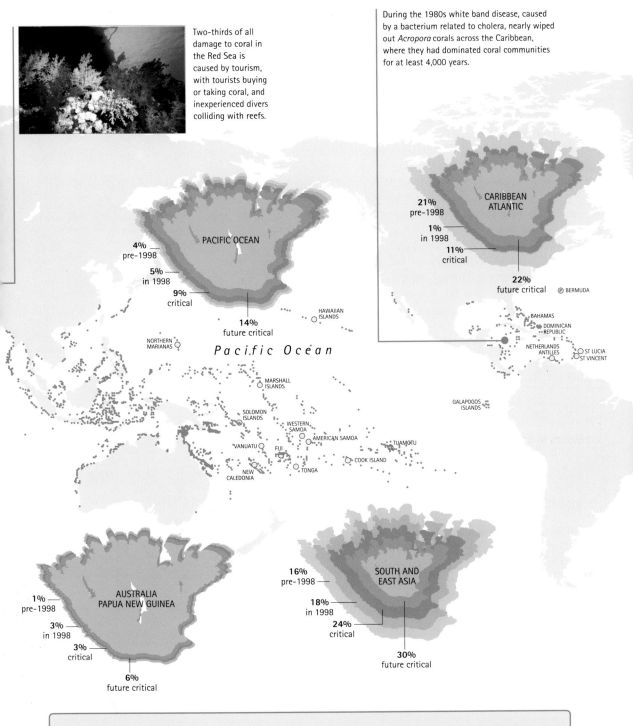

Two-thirds of all damage to coral in the Red Sea is caused by tourism, with tourists buying or taking coral, and inexperienced divers colliding with reefs.

During the 1980s white band disease, caused by a bacterium related to cholera, nearly wiped out *Acropora* corals across the Caribbean, where they had dominated coral communities for at least 4,000 years.

21%
pre-1998

1%
in 1998

11%
critical

22%
future critical

CARIBBEAN ATLANTIC

⊚ BERMUDA

BAHAMAS

DOMINICAN REPUBLIC

NETHERLANDS ANTILLES

ST LUCIA
ST VINCENT

GALAPOGOS ISLANDS

PACIFIC OCEAN

4%
pre-1998

5%
in 1998

9%
critical

14%
future critical

HAWAIIAN ISLANDS

NORTHERN MARIANAS

Pacific Ocean

MARSHALL ISLANDS

SOLOMON ISLANDS

WESTERN SAMOA

AMERICAN SAMOA

TUAMOTU

VANUATU

FIJI

COOK ISLAND

NEW CALEDONIA

TONGA

1%
pre-1998

3%
in 1998

3%
critical

6%
future critical

AUSTRALIA
PAPUA NEW GUINEA

16%
pre-1998

18%
in 1998

24%
critical

30%
future critical

SOUTH AND EAST ASIA

THE STATE OF CORAL

  coral reefs

Coral reef destroyed
percentage of total given

  before 1998

  in 1998

Coral reef expected to be destroyed in future
percentage of total given

  1998 – 2008 *projected*

  2008 – 2028 *projected*

Coral expected to remain healthy

  2028 *projected*

31

OCEANS

There could be between 500,000 and 5 million species inhabiting the dark recesses of the sea, in ecosystems that are being destroyed even before they have been discovered. This rich and varied landscape has, until recently, been largely unstudied. Only since the development of submersibles able to withstand immense pressure have some of the secrets of the ocean depths been revealed.

Plankton and the carcasses of larger animals, drawn from the surface by gravity and currents, provide one source of energy in these completely dark waters, and cold-water coral on the sea-bed survives at depths of over 6,000 feet (2,000 metres), using tree-like branching structures to capture its food. Volcanoes thrust from the thin crust under the oceans, forming "seamounts", and hydrothermal vents in the ocean floor belch out hydrogen sulphide, which microbes harness through chemosynthesis to provide another source of energy.

It is around seamounts that the most abundant deep-sea life is found. But even as these features are being identified and studied, they are being targeted by deep-sea bottom trawlers, which drag nets across the sea-bed, completely destroying any coral in its path. Around 40 percent of the world's trawling grounds are now in waters deeper than the continental shelves.

Deep-sea species tend to be long-lived and slow to reproduce, and deep-sea trawling is causing their stocks to decline. Since trawling for orange roughy started in the late 1970s, stocks of this species are thought to have fallen by more than 70 percent in more than half the areas studied. In addition to the fish targeted by the trawlers, the nets bring up many other species, such as rare deep-sea sharks. The damage to the ecosystem on which these fish and other creatures depend is irrevocable, and national governments and international organizations such as the EU and UN are urgently working to establish Marine Protected Areas.

Localized damage to, and pollution of, the seabed, is caused by drilling for oil and gas, as technology enables this to take place at ever-increasing depths. The mining of metals from the crusts that form around volcanic activity and in the form of polymetallic nodules lying on the sea-bed is in its infancy, but is likely to inflict

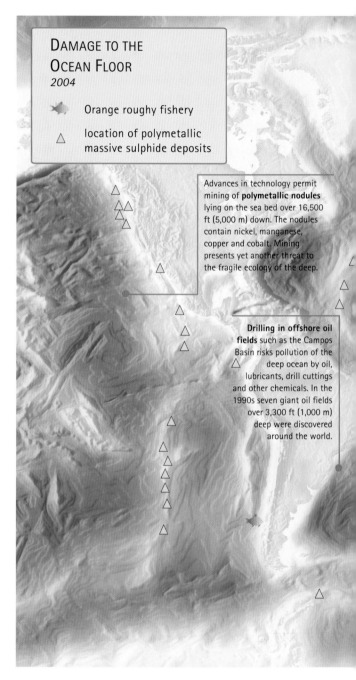

DAMAGE TO THE OCEAN FLOOR
2004

Orange roughy fishery

△ location of polymetallic massive sulphide deposits

Advances in technology permit mining of **polymetallic nodules** lying on the sea bed over 16,500 ft (5,000 m) down. The nodules contain nickel, manganese, copper and cobalt. Mining presents yet another threat to the fragile ecology of the deep.

Drilling in offshore oil fields such as the Campos Basin risks pollution of the deep ocean by oil, lubricants, drill cuttings and other chemicals. In the 1990s seven giant oil fields over 3,300 ft (1,000 m) deep were discovered around the world.

substantial damage as it develops. The increasing acidity of the oceans, caused by increased absorption of carbon dioxide from burning of fossil fuels, may also have a widespread impact on these deep waters. For example, the ability of corals to lay down calcium carbonate skeletons will be impaired.

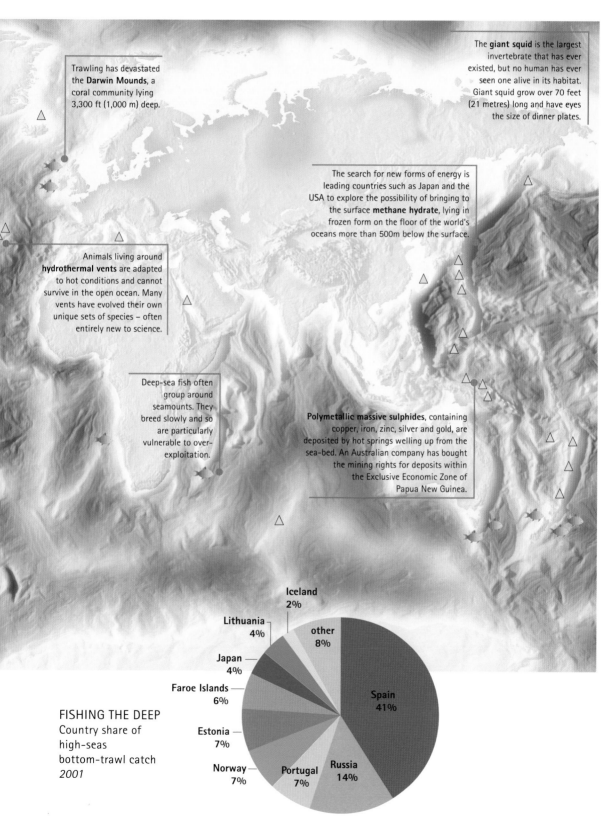

Trawling has devastated the **Darwin Mounds**, a coral community lying 3,300 ft (1,000 m) deep.

The **giant squid** is the largest invertebrate that has ever existed, but no human has ever seen one alive in its habitat. Giant squid grow over 70 feet (21 metres) long and have eyes the size of dinner plates.

The search for new forms of energy is leading countries such as Japan and the USA to explore the possibility of bringing to the surface **methane hydrate**, lying in frozen form on the floor of the world's oceans more than 500m below the surface.

Animals living around **hydrothermal vents** are adapted to hot conditions and cannot survive in the open ocean. Many vents have evolved their own unique sets of species – often entirely new to science.

Deep-sea fish often group around seamounts. They breed slowly and so are particularly vulnerable to over-exploitation.

Polymetallic massive sulphides, containing copper, iron, zinc, silver and gold, are deposited by hot springs welling up from the sea-bed. An Australian company has bought the mining rights for deposits within the Exclusive Economic Zone of Papua New Guinea.

FISHING THE DEEP
Country share of high-seas bottom-trawl catch
2001

Iceland 2%
Lithuania 4%
other 8%
Japan 4%
Faroe Islands 6%
Spain 41%
Estonia 7%
Norway 7%
Portugal 7%
Russia 14%

Total catch: 205,024 tonnes

FRAGILE REGIONS

"There are no passengers on spaceship earth.
We are all crew."

— Marshall McLuhan

35

THE ARCTIC

The Arctic presents some of the harshest conditions on the planet but is home to unique and fragile communities. Plants that are dormant for most of the year blossom during the brief Arctic summer. Vast numbers of birds, including over a hundred species of waterfowl and waders, breed and then migrate all over the world. Animals, such as polar bears, arctic foxes and seals, breed and then remain to over-winter.

Polar bears used to be widely hunted for their skins and meat. By 1970 their numbers had fallen below 10,000. In 1973 Canada, Denmark (which governs Greenland), Norway, the USA, and what was the USSR signed the International Agreement on Conservation of Polar Bears and Their Habitat. The treaty protects the polar bears' feeding and breeding grounds and their migration routes. It also bans the capture of polar bears, except by scientists working to preserve the species, and by the Inuit, who are allowed to hunt only a certain number each year, and are banned from doing so when female bears are pregnant or with their cubs.

The countries have established reserves where polar bears are completely protected. The international agreement also states that all five nations must ban polar-bear hunting from aircraft and large motorized boats, conduct and co-ordinate management and research efforts, and exchange research results and data. Since 1973 the polar bear population has risen again to between 20,000 and 40,000.

Hunting is not the only threat to Arctic wildlife. In recent years warmer Atlantic Ocean water has penetrated the Arctic Ocean basin. Arctic ice cover and salinity have declined as the ice-cap has melted. Permafrost soils in Alaska, Canada and Russia are thawing. Buildings, roads, oil pipelines and other structures built on the frozen hard soils suffer damage as a result. Whether these changes are part of a short-term natural cycle or a manifestation of global warming is the subject of intense scientific study. Shrinking sea-ice in the Arctic will cause reductions in ice algae, which live beneath the ice and form the base of the Arctic food chain. This will affect fish, seals, whales and polar bears. Polar bears are already suffering from the loss of their hunting grounds on ice-shelves. Global warming will also cause forests to move north, replacing the Arctic tundra, affecting birds, such as the critically endangered red-breasted goose (see below), that breed in the tundra.

Persistent organic pollutants (POPs) are produced by industries all over the world. They are wafted to the Arctic by wind and sea, and also by migrating animals. Arctic wildlife is exposed to DDT (a pesticide), PCBs (from electronic equipment), and dioxins (from plastics). POPs are not excreted by animals, but accumulate in their fatty tissue. Those highest up the food chain, such as seals and polar bears, are most severely exposed. These chemicals can affect fertility and damage the immune system. Heavy metals, including mercury, arsenic, and lead are also carried to the Arctic.

Collaboration between polar nations to address these wider problems is co-ordinated by the Arctic Council. The deeper causes of many of the problems facing the Arctic, such as global warming and industrial pollution, lie much further to the south, in the energy-heavy rich industrialized nations, and can only be tackled there.

RED-BREASTED GOOSE
Population in Europe
1992 – 1994
numbers

69,739
1992

73,856
1993

37,355
1994

The **Arctic National Wildlife Refuge** is a wilderness of 19 million acres, home to polar bears, wolves, lynx and vast herds of caribou. Over 100 species of migratory birds pass through the Refuge. Although protected from development since its foundation in 1960, the proposal to drill for oil on the Refuge's 1.5 million acre coastal plain presents a grave threat to its wildlife, especially the breeding caribou.

PACIFIC OCEAN

Bering Sea

Sea of Okhotsk

Gulf of Alaska

ALASKA

Chukchi Sea

Kolyma

Yukon

East Siberian Sea

RUSSIA

Lena

Mackenzie

Laptev Sea

Saskatchewan

CANADA

ARCTIC OCEAN
North Pole

Kara Sea

Hudson Bay

Baffin Bay

Barents Sea

Pechora

GREENLAND

Greenland Sea

Arctic Circle

GREENLAND

Volga

Rising temperatures and earlier spring melts could expose polar bear cubs, born in snow dens, to the harsh cold of the Arctic too early in their development.

ICELAND

Norwegian Sea

NORWAY

SWEDEN

FINLAND

ATLANTIC OCEAN

Protected Areas

scientific reserve

national, provincial or territorial park

nature reserve or wildlife sanctuary

A pipeline in the Komi Republic of Russia ruptured in September 1994, spilling 100,000 tonnes of oil. A major clean-up operation prevented widespread ecological damage in the Pechora river basin, but aging pipes and poor maintenance could lead to another tragedy.

THE ANTARCTIC

The Antarctic is a continent larger than Europe, measuring 5.4 million square miles (14 million sq kms). Temperatures rarely rise above freezing, and most of the land is covered in ice. Glaciers flow from the interior into the oceans, creating enormous, half-mile thick ice-shelves.

Life flourishes despite these severe conditions. Mosses and lichens grow around the coasts and on the islands, and tiny worms and other invertebrates live on the land. In Antarctic waters microscopic plankton provide food for small crustaceans called krill, which in turn are eaten by fish, seabirds, and mammals.

Argentina, Australia, Chile, France, New Zealand, Norway, and the UK have all laid claim to parts of the Antarctic, although their sovereignty is not recognized by most other nations. The 1959 Antarctic Treaty promotes scientific co-operation and prohibits military activity, such as weapons testing, and waste dumping. Participating countries designate Specially Protected Areas (see map), to which access is restricted in order to leave important wildlife features undisturbed. Until the mid-1980s scientific bases created high levels of local contamination (waste products, oil and rubbish). More recently, the scientific community has realized the importance of maintaining the Antarctic in its pristine state, as far as possible.

Their attempts may be in vain, however, if the changes observed on the Antarctic peninsula, where temperatures have risen by around 2.5°C since the 1950s, turn out to be a precursor of a more general warming. Maybe the most dramatic event has been the disintegration of the majority of the 220-metre thick Larsen B ice shelf. It had already lost 2,500 sq km by early 2002 when a further 3,250 sq km broke off in just 35 days. The loss of sea ice around the peninsula has decimated the Adélie penguins, which use it to reach their feeding grounds. As their numbers dwindle, they are being replaced by gentoo penguins, which thrive in open waters.

There are also reports that the number of krill, on which so many species depend, had declined in 2003 to just one-fifth of their level in the 1970s. Krill feed on algae that form under sea ice, and so will be affected by its diminishing area. They are also likely to be adversely affected by the increase in ultraviolet radiation resulting from the hole in the stratospheric ozone layer above Antarctica, caused largely by the industrial emission of chlorofluorocarbons (CFCs).

The effects of climate change are among many subjects being studied by the scientists working in the region. The terrain serves as a living laboratory. The lichens growing on the rocks of the cold, dry valleys of Victoria Land, for example, give vital clues to life in severe conditions, such as those millions of years ago on Mars. Studies of the relationship between populations of natural predators and their prey in the seas surrounding the continent may lead to better management of fisheries worldwide.

Commercial krill fishing began in the 1970s, but fears of over-exploitation led to the Convention on the Conservation of Antarctic Marine Living Resources in 1981. This restricts the total annual krill catch, which is now about 130,000 tonnes. Antarctic ice-fish and fin-fish have also been exploited and their numbers have dwindled. Illegal fishing boats may be responsible for five times more fish being landed than the reported 120,000 tonnes, and are certainly breaking the ban on whaling within the Southern Ocean Sanctuary (see opposite).

Threatened Antarctic species include the **Rockhopper** and **Macaroni penguins**, several types of albatross (Amsterdam, Wandering, Indian Yellow-nosed, Grey-headed, Salvin's and Sooty), the Southern Giant and White-chinned petrels, the Eaton's Pintail duck, and the Blue and Fin whales.

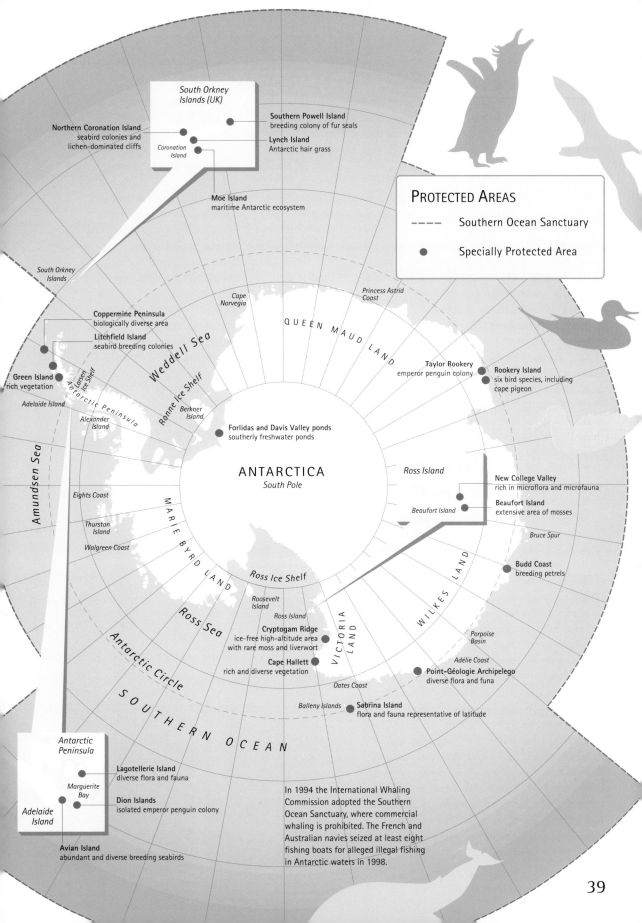

South Orkney Islands (UK)

Northern Coronation Island
seabird colonies and
lichen-dominated cliffs

Coronation Island

Southern Powell Island
breeding colony of fur seals

Lynch Island
Antarctic hair grass

Moe Island
maritime Antarctic ecosystem

PROTECTED AREAS

- - - - - Southern Ocean Sanctuary

● Specially Protected Area

South Orkney Islands

Cape Norvegia

Princess Astrid Coast

QUEEN MAUD LAND

Coppermine Peninsula
biologically diverse area

Litchfield Island
seabird breeding colonies

Green Island
rich vegetation

Weddell Sea

Larsen Ice Shelf

Antarctic Peninsula

Ronne Ice Shelf

Berkner Island

Adelaide Island

Alexander Island

Taylor Rookery
emperor penguin colony

Rookery Island
six bird species, including
cape pigeon

Forlidas and Davis Valley ponds
southerly freshwater ponds

ANTARCTICA
South Pole

Ross Island

New College Valley
rich in microflora and microfauna

Beaufort Island
extensive area of mosses

Beaufort Island

Bruce Spur

Amundsen Sea

Eights Coast

Thurston Island

Walgreen Coast

MARIE BYRD LAND

Ross Ice Shelf

Roosevelt Island

Ross Island

WILKES LAND

Budd Coast
breeding petrels

Porpoise Basin

Ross Sea

Antarctic Circle

Cryptogam Ridge
ice-free high-altitude area
with rare moss and liverwort

Cape Hallett
rich and diverse vegetation

VICTORIA LAND

Oates Coast

Adélie Coast

Point-Géologie Archipelego
diverse flora and funa

SOUTHERN OCEAN

Balleny Islands

Sabrina Island
flora and fauna representative of latitude

Antarctic Peninsula

Lagotellerie Island
diverse flora and fauna

Marguerite Bay

Dion Islands
isolated emperor penguin colony

Adelaide Island

Avian Island
abundant and diverse breeding seabirds

In 1994 the International Whaling
Commission adopted the Southern
Ocean Sanctuary, where commercial
whaling is prohibited. The French and
Australian navies seized at least eight
fishing boats for alleged illegal fishing
in Antarctic waters in 1998.

AUSTRALIA

At 3 million square miles (8 million sq km), Australia is the world's smallest continent. Yet its terrain is incredibly diverse, ranging from its central deserts to the rainforests of Queensland and Tasmania. The unique plant and animal life found in Australia is a reflection of its geographical isolation. Marsupials, or pouched mammals, such as the kangaroo or koala, have evolved into species as diverse as foetal mammals elsewhere in the world.

In an attempt to preserve Australia's rich biodiversity Unesco has designated a number of World Heritage Sites. Although some of these are recognized for their fossils, most have been awarded their special status because of the need to protect unique natural habitats.

Australia's flora and fauna are sensitive both to climate changes and to those brought about by humans. Some 34 species of animal are known to have become extinct in the past 30,000 years. The extinctions prior to the arrival of European settlers in the late 18th century were largely caused by an inadequate and fluctuating water supplies. More recent extinctions – of the Tasmanian tiger and several species of wallaby and bandicoot, for example – have been caused by humans.

Since their arrival in the late 18th century, European settlers have cleared and cultivated land in Australia, resulting in damage to more than 35 percent of the country's woodland, and the loss of up to 75 percent of the rainforest. Tree felling has led to soil erosion, and to the water table rising, which increases the salinity of the soil and destroys any trees left standing. New trees have been introduced but this has not helped: some of these cause further damage. The native pastures of Queensland, for example, have been turned into scrubland by the non-native prickly acacia.

Animal species that have been introduced have also wreaked havoc. The natural habitats of indigenous birds and marsupials have been disturbed by grazing cattle and sheep. Aggressive hunters such as the fox (introduced by European sportsmen as quarry) kill indigenous species, as well as the non-native rabbit. The cane toad, introduced as a pest-control measure, has itself turned into a pest.

The Great Barrier Reef lies off the coast of Queensland. The product of early changes in sea level followed by subsidence, this is one of the ecological wonders of the world. It is over 1,250 miles (2,000 km) long, with a total area of 135,100 square miles (350,000 sq km). It was made a World Heritage Site in 1981. As one of Australia's major tourist attractions government agencies and environmental groups are having to work hard to protect it from the ravages inflicted by its hundreds of thousands of visitors.

In 1999 the Australian government enacted the Environment Protection and Biodiversity Conservation Act, which introduced a comprehensive national protection scheme for wildlife. Rigorous assessment and approval is required for any building development likely to affect the habitats of threatened or migratory species. Time will tell whether these measures will reverse the decline of Australia's wildlife.

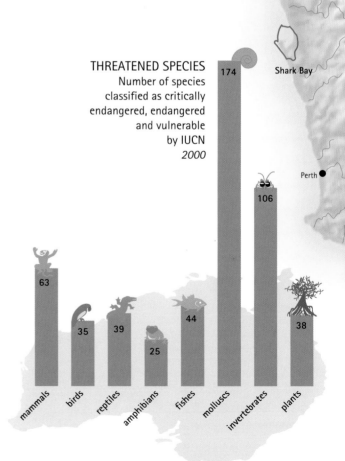

THREATENED SPECIES
Number of species classified as critically endangered, endangered and vulnerable by IUCN
2000

Shark Bay

Perth

Category	Number
mammals	63
birds	35
reptiles	39
amphibians	25
fishes	44
molluscs	174
invertebrates	106
plants	38

Once, large flocks of **Gouldian Finches** were a common sight in northern Australia. Changes in land management, such as the rising frequency of fires and competition with cattle, have reduced the availability of native grass seed that Gouldian Finches eat. Now only a few small, scattered populations remain.

DEGREE OF THREAT
Number of threatened plants and animals in each IUCN Red List category
2000

48 critically endangered

128 endangered

348 vulnerable

Darwin
Kakadu National Park

Roper

Fitzroy

Tanami Desert

Great Sandy Desert

Northern Australia

Simpson Desert

Gibson Desert

Alice Springs

Uluru-Kata Tjuta National Park

Great Victoria Desert

South Australia

Mitchell

Wet Tropics of Queensland

Australian Fossil Mammal Site (Riversleigh)

Great Barrier Reef

Great Dividing Range

Queensland

Fraser Island

Brisbane

Central Eastern Rainforest Reserves Of Australia

Darling

New South Wales

The Greater Blue Mountains Area

Sydney

Willandra Lake Region

Adelaide

Murray

CANBERRA

Australian Fossil Mammal Site (Naracoorte)

Victoria

Melbourne

Lord Howe Island

Macquarie Island

Heard and McDonald Islands

WORLD HERITAGE SITES

— boundary of World Heritage Site

• smaller World Heritage Site

Orange-bellied parakeets are endemic to the island of Tasmania. Only about 200 remain. Although its summer breeding ground is protected, orange-bellied parakeets over-winter on mainland Australia, where their habitat has been damaged by grazing. A captive breeding program began in 1986.

Tasmania

Hobart

Tasmanian Wilderness

41

Central and South America is the most biologically diverse landmass in the world. It includes temperate and tropical forests, high-altitude desert plateau, and the glacial peaks of the Andes. While some areas remain relatively untouched by humans, others have been decimated by rapid urban growth. Last-ditch attempts are being made to save the Atlantic forests of Brazil, home to numerous species of plants and animals found nowhere else in the world, but reduced to less than 8 percent of their original size. Natural World Heritage Sites have been established throughout the continent but in 2001 three of these were on the "danger list" as a result of poor administration.

Important ecological areas do not fit neatly within political boundaries, and conservation projects are increasingly seeking co-operation between countries. In Central America, for example, where there are more than 400 protected areas, efforts are being made to establish a "Mesoamerican biological corridor" that integrates the efforts of eight countries. Although forest and mountain areas are now fairly well protected, more needs to be done to conserve wetland, coastal and marine areas. International co-operation is not always forthcoming. Attempts to protect the biologically rich mountainous Cordillera del Condor region in South America, for example, have been hampered by a border dispute between Ecuador and Peru.

It is important to protect the ecology of the high Andes region because its destruction or pollution would have an adverse effect on the water supply for the Amazon river. The Amazon basin itself contains the largest rainforest in the world and is home to several million species of plants, animals (including 3,000 species of fish) and micro-organisms, many of which remain unrecorded. The relatively stable climate, with high humidity and steady temperatures, has enabled species to adapt to local conditions and occupy very narrow environmental niches. The result is a large number of species, but a higher risk of a single species becoming extinct with the destruction of its own particular corner of the Amazon.

Indigenous peoples subsist in the Amazon by hunting, gathering and farming. Despite the luxuriant vegetation, the soils of the Amazon are sandy and infertile, so yields of staple crops such as cassava are low. This fragile food supply, coupled with the problems presented by moving through the forest, has given rise to small, diverse tribes living far apart from each other. The arrival of Europeans brought cattle ranching and the timber industry. Initially, settlement was restricted to the banks of the navigable rivers, still the principal means of transport, but the Trans-Amazon Highway, built in the 1960s, opened the interior of the Amazon to development. Once rainforest has been cleared for logging and to create pasture, it is prone to erosion. The extent of the loss of rainforest habitat is contested, but the latest estimates are that 14 percent of the total forest area was lost during the 20th century. In addition, mining effluent, which can contain mercury, has severely polluted parts of the Amazon River.

In 2001 the Brazilian Government announced an infrastructure program for the region, called "Advance Brazil" to encourage soya farming and its export. It includes plans for 6,250 miles (10,000 km) of new or upgraded roads through the rainforest, as well as canals to bypass the Amazon's rapids. Roads attract settlers and loggers, and substantially increase the risk of forest fires. Scientists predict that 42 percent of the rainforest could be denuded or degraded by 2020.

Opponents to the scheme argue that other, more sustainable, approaches to harnessing the resources of the Amazon could have been provided by eco-tourism, sensitive forestry and the study of practical uses for natural products and the genetic information contained in the region's wildlife. Loss of this habitat will not only exacerbate global warming, as the rainforest goes up in smoke, it will also deny Brazil an opportunity to sell "carbon credits" to industrialized countries unwilling to reduce their domestic emissions of carbon dioxide.

Whale Sanctuary of El Vizcaino

MEXICO

Sian Ka'an
Barrier-Reef Reserve System
Tikal National Park

CUBA

JAMAICA

DOMINICAN REPUBLIC
HAITI

Morne Trois Pitons National Park

DOMINICA

GUATEMALA
BELIZE
Río Platano Biosphere Reserve
EL SALVADOR
HONDURAS
NICARAGUA
COSTA RICA
PANAMA

Area De Conservación Guanacaste
Darien National Park
Los Katios National Park

COCOS ISLAND
Cocos Island National Park

GALAPAGOS ISLANDS
Galapagos Islands

ECUADOR
Sangay National Park

PERU
Huascarán National Park
Manu National Park

VENEZUELA

COLOMBIA

TRINIDAD & TOBAGO
GUYANA
SURINAME

Canaima National Park

Central Suriname Nature Reserve

B R A Z I L

Jaú National Park
Panatal Conservation Area
Noel Kempff Mercado National Park

BOLIVIA

PARAGUAY

Discovery Coast Atlantic Forest Reserves

Atlantic Forest Southeast Reserves

Iguacu National Park
Iguazu National Park

CHILE

URUGUAY

ARGENTINA

Península Valdés

Los Glaciares

PROTECTED LAND
Percentage of total land area protected under IUCN categories I-V *1997*

- 36% – 45%
- 21% – 35%
- 11% – 20%
- 1% – 10%
- under 1.0%
- none or no data
- ● World Heritage Site
- ◉ World Heritage Site on danger list in *2001*

It is predicted that the proposed new road from Cuiabá to Santarem will carry 20 million tons of crops to the river, and that it will create a corridor of development up to 60 miles (100 km) wide.

Around 55% of the trees and 80% of the primates found in Brazil's Atlantic forest, including the **muriqui**, are endemic to the area.

In 1998 and 1999 **fires** ravaged the Amazon. They destroyed 30% of crops in the Brazilian state of Roraima and threatened indigenous Indian villages.

COLOMBIA
Boa Vista
Macapá
Belém

ECUADOR

PERU
Rio Amazonas
Manaus
Santarém
Maraba

Humaitá
Pôrto Velho
Rio Branco

Rio Tapajós

BRAZIL

Brasília

Cuiabá

BOLIVIA

AMAZON BASIN

- ▨ IUCN Protected Areas categories I – VI
- ⊟ Tapajos National Park
- — existing road
- ━ proposed upgraded road

The **Tapajos National Park**, set up in 1974, covers about 3,860 square miles (10,000 sq km) of dense tropical rain forest, home to abundant wildlife. The proposal to upgrade the Trans-Amazon highway is bound to have a derimental effect on the ecology of the park.

GALAPAGOS ISLANDS

The Galapagos Islands lie in the Pacific Ocean, about 625 miles (1,000 km) off the coast of South America. Because these volcanic islands have risen out of the seabed, evolution has taken place in isolation from the mainland, giving rise to species endemic to the islands. As Charles Darwin realized after his visit in 1835, species on neighbouring islands within the group have evolved unique characteristics in response to their environment. The result is small, localized populations that are vulnerable to habitat destruction, disease, or climate change.

"Galapagos" means "tortoise" in Spanish, and the islands are home to giant tortoises, as well as about 300,000 marine iguanas. In the absence of traditional predators – rice rats and two species of bat are the only native mammals – seabirds breed freely and colonies of boobies, frigate birds, and the rare lava gull flourish on the islands. In 1959 Ecuador declared the Galapagos a national park and in 1978 the islands became the first United Nations' World Heritage Site.

Some of the islands have been settled by humans, and the population had reached over 16,000 in 2001. Settlers have imported around 500 species of plants, which are displacing the native flora, as well as non-native animals, such as goats, which compete for grazing land with the giant tortoises.

Tourism is the mainstay of the islands' economy, with over 60,000 tourists visiting each year. Fishing is also important, with at least 800 fishermen based on the islands. Large, commercial boats also fish offshore, creating a hazard to marine mammals and birds.

Prompted by Unesco's threat to place the Galapagos on the World Heritage in Danger list, Ecuador issued an emergency decree in 1997 restricting the introduction of alien species, and promoting conservation. In 1998 Ecuador expanded the islands' no-fishing zone from 15 to 40 nautical miles offshore. However, attempts to limit fishing have met with local resistance. Park wardens have been shot, giant tortoises taken hostage and a research station damaged. The fate of the islands' wildlife hangs on whether both local and conservational needs can be met.

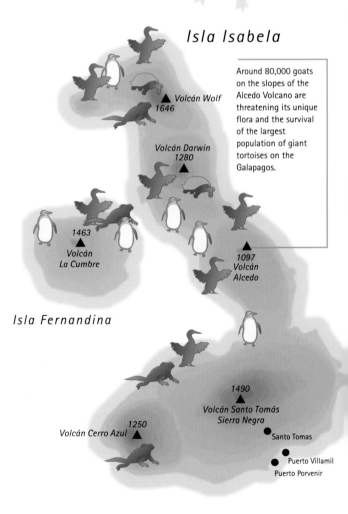

The **Galapagos penguin** is at risk. These penguins eat fish, abundant in the cold, nutrient-rich waters around the islands. Many suffered as a result of the El Niño phenomenon in 1997–98, when warmer seas disrupted the penguins' food supply.

Isla Isabela

Around 80,000 goats on the slopes of the Alcedo Volcano are threatening its unique flora and the survival of the largest population of giant tortoises on the Galapagos.

▲ Volcán Wolf
1646

Volcán Darwin
1280 ▲

1463 ▲
Volcán
La Cumbre

1097
Volcán
Alcedo

Isla Fernandina

1490 ▲
Volcán Santo Tomás
Sierra Negra

1250
Volcán Cerro Azul ▲

● Santo Tomas

● Puerto Villamil
● Puerto Porvenir

Found only on the Galapagos, the **lava gull**, with 300 to 400 breeding pairs, is considered the rarest gull in the world.

Isla Pinta

Isla Marchena

Isla Genovesa

The **giant tortoise**, once numerous on the islands, presented an easy meal to passing sailors and three of the 14 known subspecies became extinct. In recent times, the main threat to the tortoise has been the domestic goat, which competes with it for grazing. Captive-breeding projects have been running since the mid-1960s. These are too late, however, for "Lonesome George", the sole remaining tortoise from the island of Pinta.

GIANT TORTOISE
Estimated number
of individuals in
1535 and *2000*

250,000   **15,000**

1535   *2000*

Isla San Salvador

Isla Rábida

Isla Santa Cruz

On 16 January 2001, the oil tanker *Jessica*, carrying 160,000 gallons of diesel and 80,000 gallons of bunker fuel, ran aground off San Cristóbal Island. Her tanks ruptured. Fortunately, winds and currents took the oil away from the island, preventing a major ecological disaster.

Isla Pinzón

Since 1970 more than 500 young tortoises, bred in captivity, have been released on the island of Pinzon.

● Puerto Ayora

Isla Santa Fé

Puerto Baquerizo Moreno ●   ● El Progreso

Between the mid-1960s and 1974, 14 giant tortoises, whose grazing had been decimated by goats, were taken from Española to breeding pens on Santa Cruz island. The goats were eventually removed from the island and by March 2000 a total of 1,000 tortoises had been reintroduced to the island.

Isla San Cristóbal

Puerto Velasco Ibarra ●

Isla Santa María

Isla Española

MADAGASCAR

Madagascar is the world's fourth largest island, with a land area of approximately 226,000 square miles (582,000 sq km). It is thought to have separated from Gondwanaland (present-day Africa) 60 million years ago.

Madagascar's geographical isolation has led to separate evolution, producing many endemic species and a diverse range of habitat: tropical conditions along the coast, temperate inland areas and arid deserts in the south.

Several of Madagascar's endemic species are threatened, despite the government's endorsement of international agreements on biodiversity, desertification, endangered species, and marine life conservation. With a human population exceeding 14 million and growing at an annual rate of nearly 3 percent, the pressure on the country's natural habitats is likely to continue.

Although the great elephantbird and Delalande's coua, or snail-eating coua, are known to have become extinct, new species are being discovered all the time. A new species of woolly lemur, five new dwarf lemurs and three more species of mouse lemur were all announced at the end of 2000, bringing the total number of known lemur species to sixty-one.

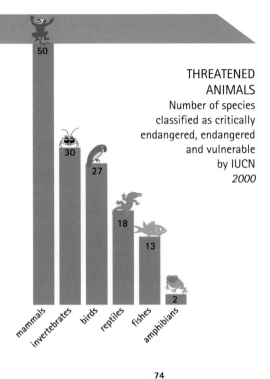

THREATENED ANIMALS
Number of species classified as critically endangered, endangered and vulnerable by IUCN
2000

50 mammals
30 invertebrates
27 birds
18 reptiles
13 fishes
2 amphibians

DEGREE OF THREAT
Number of animals in each IUCN Red List category
2000

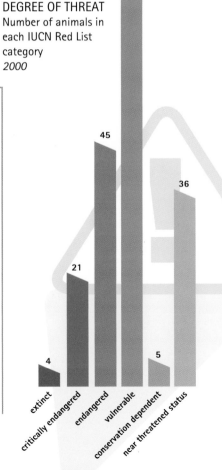

4 extinct
21 critically endangered
45 endangered
74 vulnerable
5 conservation dependent
36 near threatened status

THREATENED PLANT SPECIES
Number of threatened plants
2000

0 extinct
19 possibly extinct
93 endangered
57 vulnerable
90 rare
64 indeterminate

The **Madagascar rosy periwinkle** is the source of two alkaloids — vincristine and vinblastine — used to treat (and usually cure) childhood leukaemia. The plants from which the alkaloids are extracted are now grown elsewhere. The drug industry has not returned any benefit to the people or to conservation projects in Madagascar.

The **fish eagle** was common in north-west Madagascar until the 1930s. It is now very rare, as a result of persecution, hunting, and the loss of nesting and feeding habitat.

Tsingy de Bermaraha Strict Nature Reserve is a World Heritage Site. Endangered lemurs and birds thrive in the undisturbed forests, lakes and mangrove swamps.

The **golden lemur**, or golden bamboo lemur, has a range restricted to south-eastern Madagascar. About 1,000 inhabit the Ranomafana National Park. They live in rain forest, eating the base of bamboo leaves and all new growth. The young bamboo shoots eaten by the golden lemur are toxic and lethal to most other mammals.

Cap d'Ambre
Antsiranana
Forêt d'Ambre
Montagne d'Ambre
Analamerana
Ankarana
Iharana
Lokobe
Tsaratanana
Manongarlvo
Andapa
Marojejy
Bora
Anjanaharibe-Sud
Antalaha
Masoala
Nosy Mangabe
Mahajanga
Sofia
Marovoay
Katsepy
Ankarafantsika
Cap Saint-André
Lac Kinkony
Baie Baly/Soalaid
Tampoketsa Analamaitso
Mananara
Tsingy de Namoroka
Marotandrano
Ambalovaky
Maningozo
Lac Alaotra
Fenoarivo Atsinanana
Bemarivo
Manambaho
Katsijy
Zahamena
Ambohijanahary
Betampona
Ambohitartely
Mangerivola
Toamasina
Bemaraha
Mantadia
Manambolo
Antananarivo
Lac Bemamba
Lac Itasy
Antsirabe
Mangoro
Kirindy
Morondava
Ancranomena
Ranomafana
Fianarantsoa
Mananjary
Mangoky
orombe
Lac Ihotry
Andringitra
Zombitse
Isalo
Andrevo
Vohibasia
Pic de Ivohibe
Toliara
Onilahy
Manombo
Beza-Mahafaly
Kalambatritra
Tsimanampetsotsa
Andohahela
Hatokaliotsy
Taolanaro
Lac Anony
Cap Sainte-Marie

Mahavay
Ikopa
Betsiboka

PROTECTED AREAS IN MADAGASCAR

⭑ Strict Nature Reserve

☆ National Park

● Habitat Species Management Are

● Managed Resource Protected Are

ENDANGERED ANIMALS AND PLANTS

4

"Thousands of cooking pots across Africa are simmering away with cuts of gorilla and chimp in them."

— Sam Kanyamibwa,
World Conservation Monitoring Centre, Rwanda

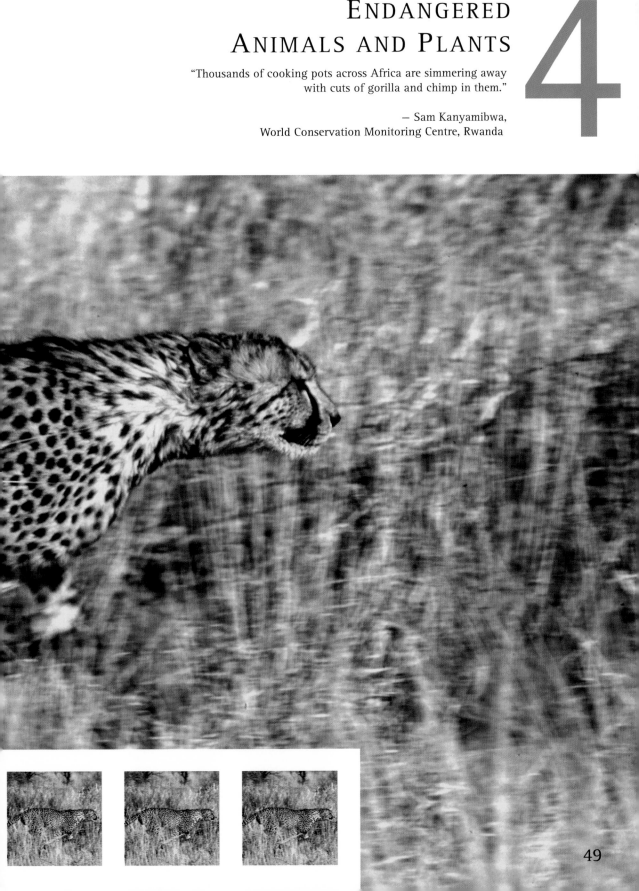

PRIMATES

Apes, humans, monkeys, and prosimians such as lorises, bush babies, and lemurs make up the 234 species of Primates, a mammalian Order with distinctive common features indicating descent from a single ancestor: a small, tree-dwelling mammal that subsisted primarily on insects.

Primates have prehensile hands with opposable thumbs, large brains (especially the cerebral cortex), and usually bear single offspring. Most are well adapted to life in trees, especially tropical forests, although some species have become terrestrial. Primates tend to live in complex social groups, and as infants are dependent on their mother, both for sustanance and for lessons in the practical and social skills. With a few exceptions, such as the Japanese macaque that lives on the Shimokita Peninsula at a latitude of 41°N, very few primates have colonized temperate areas because they need a supply of food during the winter months as well as long daylight hours for foraging.

All primates share behavioral and anatomical characteristics, but humans and chimpanzees are particularly close. Chimps share almost 99 percent of our DNA. They use tools, laugh when tickled, and – when allowed – can live for 60 years. Like many other species of primate, chimps are endangered by deforestation and, especially, its consequences: as logging companies open up the forests, hunters move in. Since the mid-1980s hunting for "bushmeat" has become a lucrative industry. In 2001, over a million tonnes was taken from the Congo basin alone.

A hundred years ago there were some two million chimps living in the Central African rainforest, stretching from Sierra Leone to Tanzania. In 2001 only 200,000 remained; at the current rates of decline they all could perish by 2010.

Our closest relatives are the four great apes: **gorilla**, chimpanzee, bonobo (pygmy chimpanzee), and orang-utan.

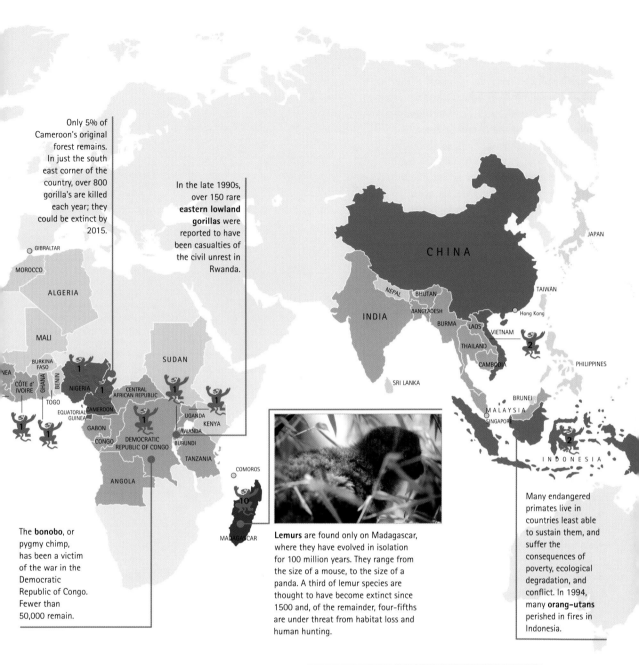

Only 5% of Cameroon's original forest remains. In just the south east corner of the country, over 800 gorilla's are killed each year; they could be extinct by 2015.

In the late 1990s, over 150 rare **eastern lowland gorillas** were reported to have been casualties of the civil unrest in Rwanda.

GIBRALTAR

MOROCCO

ALGERIA

MALI

BURKINA
FASO

NEA

CÔTE d'
IVOIRE

GHANA

BENIN

TOGO

NIGERIA 1

EQUATORIAL
GUINEA

CAMEROON 1

GABON

CONGO

CENTRAL
AFRICAN REPUBLIC

1

SUDAN

1

UGANDA

KENYA

RWANDA

DEMOCRATIC
REPUBLIC OF CONGO

1

BURUNDI

TANZANIA

ANGOLA

COMOROS

MADAGASCAR

10

CHINA

JAPAN

NEPAL

BHUTAN

TAIWAN

BANGLADESH

Hong Kong

INDIA

BURMA

LAOS

VIETNAM

2

THAILAND

CAMBODIA

PHILIPPINES

SRI LANKA

BRUNEI

MALAYSIA

SINGAPORE

INDONESIA

2

The **bonobo**, or pygmy chimp, has been a victim of the war in the Democratic Republic of Congo. Fewer than 50,000 remain.

Lemurs are found only on Madagascar, where they have evolved in isolation for 100 million years. They range from the size of a mouse, to the size of a panda. A third of lemur species are thought to have become extinct since 1500 and, of the remainder, four-fifths are under threat from habitat loss and human hunting.

Many endangered primates live in countries least able to sustain them, and suffer the consequences of poverty, ecological degradation, and conflict. In 1994, many **orang-utans** perished in fires in Indonesia.

About 90 percent of **primates** live in tropical forests. They play an integral role in the ecology of their habitat, helping to pollinate plants and disperse seeds.

THREATENED PRIMATES

Number of species of primates classified as critically endangered, endangered or vulnerable *2000*

■	more than 25
■	11 – 25
■	4 – 10
■	1 – 3
□	none or no data
🐵	number of primates classified as critically endangered

51

BIG CATS

Big cats belong to the *Felidae* family – a group of carnivorous mammals that includes the cheetah in addition to "true" cats: the lion, tiger, jaguar, leopard, puma, and the domestic cat.

Cats, whether large or small, are built for performance and are more specialized in this respect than any other flesh-eating mammal. They are powerfully built animals, with large and highly developed brains, making them more intelligent as well as stronger than their prey. They are also so well-coordinated that they almost always land on their feet when they fall.

Although the lion, tiger, and cheetah are agile climbers, they are mainly terrestrial in habit. The leopard, jaguar, and ocelot, in contrast, are very much at home in trees, where they sometimes sleep. The larger cats range over wide areas, often up to 50 square miles (129 sq km). Big cats usually rove alone or with a companion. African lions do form prides but these loosely bound groups of females, cubs and one or a few adult males lack the rigid hierarchy found in dog and wolf packs.

Humans are the main threat to big cats and hunting has long been a popular pastime. It remains a lucrative sport: in Botswana, for example, recreational hunters may pay up to US $30,000 to shoot a lion. The skin, teeth and claws of big cats provide rich pickings for traders. Those not threatened by hunters have had their extensive territories steadily eroded by agriculture and human settlement.

Many of Asia's big cats are under threat, including the snow leopard (reduced to around 6,000 in the wild), the Siberian tiger (reduced to 400 in the wild) and the Amur leopard (see page 95). As wild populations of big cats decline towards extinction, zoos and other sanctuaries become even more vital in ensuring their survival.

CANADA

UNITED STATES
OF AMERICA

MEXICO

The highly endangered **Florida Panther** is making its last stand in the higher elevations in the swamps of the Everglades. The few remaining animals became highly inbred, causing such genetic flaws as heart defects and sterility. In the 1990s, closely related panthers from Texas were released in Florida and are successfully breeding with the Florida panthers. Increased genetic variation and protection of habitat may yet save this subspecies.

WE
SA

SENEGAL —
GAMBIA —
GUINEA-BISSAU —

SIERI
LEOI

PERU

BOLIVIA

CHILE   ARGENTINA

The **cheetah** is generally considered the speediest of animals, capable of 60-70 mph (100-110 kmph), with rare reports of even higher speeds. A cheetah may also pursue its prey for a considerable distance, as much as 3.5 miles (5.5 km). But even its speed may not save it from hunters and the threat of extinction.

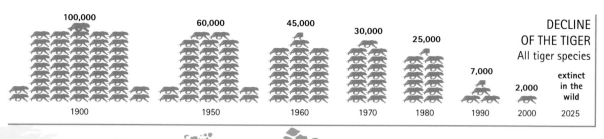

DECLINE OF THE TIGER
All tiger species

100,000	60,000	45,000	30,000	25,000	7,000	2,000	extinct in the wild
1900	1950	1960	1970	1980	1990	2000	2025

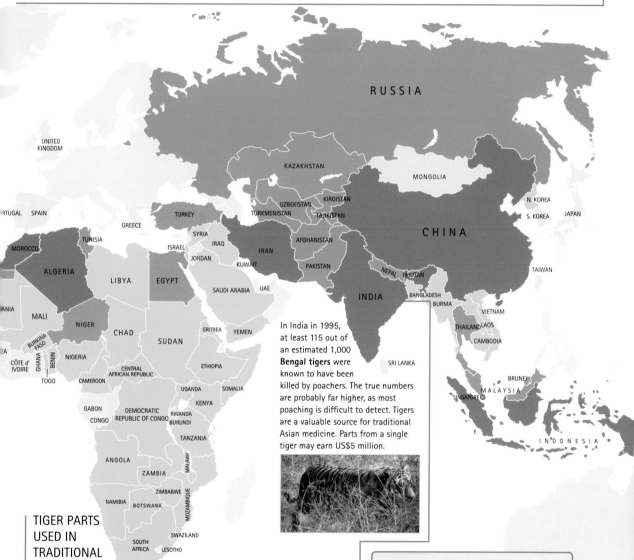

In India in 1995, at least 115 out of an estimated 1,000 **Bengal tigers** were known to have been killed by poachers. The true numbers are probably far higher, as most poaching is difficult to detect. Tigers are a valuable source for traditional Asian medicine. Parts from a single tiger may earn US$5 million.

TIGER PARTS USED IN TRADITIONAL MEDICINE

brain
laziness, pimples

eyeballs
epilepsy, malaria, fevers, cataracts, convulsions

claws
as a sedative

nose
epilepsy, convulsions, dog bites

whiskers
toothache

blood
constitution, willpower

testes
tuberculosis of the lymph nodes

tail
skin diseases

teeth
fever, rabies, asthma, sores on the penis

stomach
stomach upsets

fat
leprosy, rheumatism

bones
rheumatism, weakness, paralysis

feces
boils, piles

flesh
nausea, malaria, improves vitality, tones stomach and spleen

THREATENED CATS
Number of species of big cats classified as critically endangered, endangered or vulnerable *2000*

- 5 or more
- 4
- 3
- 2
- 1
- none or no data

53

UNGULATES

Horses, deer, cattle, pigs, sheep and goats are all ungulates – mammals with hooves of hard skin that allow the animals to run. Elephants and rhinoceroses (see pages 56-57) are also ungulates. Their teeth are adapted for their plant diet, with strong molars for grinding. Preyed upon by big cats, wolves and other carnivores, ungulates rely on various methods of defence. Some are large, many are swift, and others grow horns or antlers. They often mass in large herds to minimize the risk to an individual.

Domesticated ungulates accompanied earlier European explorers to Australia and to isolated islands all over the world, but have often threatened indigenous herbivores by over-grazing native plants. Non-native ungulates have interbred with indigenous species, and have also transmitted diseases such as rinderpest, which spreads from cattle to wild buffalo in Southeast Asia.

Ungulates provide an important source of meat for humans, and their hides are used for clothing and shelter. As vehicles and guns improved during the 20th century, ungulate populations began to suffer from the over-hunting that remains the most serious threat to their survival today.

Areas designated as reserves are often vital for ungulate conservation. The tourists flocking to witness herds of ungulates roaming over African plains, provide a potential source of income for conservation in reserves. Kruger National Park in South Africa is Africa's oldest reserve, founded in 1898, while Tanzania boasts the Serengeti and Ngorongoro parks.

To secure local support for conservation inside and outside reserves local people must enjoy the profits from hunting and tourism and participate in the management of their wildlife. The Communal Area Management Programme for Indigenous Resources (CAMPFIRE) in Zimbabwe is a successful example, demonstrating that the managed re-introduction of ungulates to areas where they had been hunted to local extinction can be successful with proper enforcement against poaching.

There may have been 60 million **bison** in North America before the arrival of Europeans. Hunting drove the bison to the point of extinction as settlers swept west across the continent. About 1,500 survived in areas such as Yellowstone National Park, established in 1872. The number of bison has since risen to over 350,000, most reared commercially for meat, hide and other products.

C A N A D A

UNITED STATES
OF AMERICA

MEXICO

BELIZE
GUATEMALA   HONDURAS
NICARAGUA
COSTA RICA
PANAMA   VENEZUELA
COLOMBIA
ECUADOR

PERU   B R A Z I L

BOLIVIA

PARAGUAY

CHILE
ARGENTINA

WESTERN
SAHARA

MAURITAN
SENEGAL —
GAMBIA —
GUINEA-BISSAU —
SIERRA LEONE —
LIBERIA —

CHANGING FORTUNES OF
THE NORTH AMERICAN BISON

1.4 million

364,000

30 – 60 million
circa 1800

1,500
circa 1900

2000

projected 2010

Only 20,000 are wild.
The rest are reared
for their meat.

Przewalski's wild horse lived in the Mongolian steppes. Wolves and humans drove it to extinction in the wild but it has recently been re-introduced.

This baby **pygmy hog** is one of 70 reared at the Durrell Wildlife Conservation Trust breeding centre in Basistha, India. The species was feared extinct, but it is hoped that a conservation recovery program will enable hogs to be reintroduced into the Himalayan foothills.

RUSSIA

UNITED KINGDOM
LITH
POLAND BELARUS
FRANCE
UKRAINE
MOLDOVA
ROMANIA
KAZAKHSTAN
MONGOLIA
N. KOREA
S. KOREA JAPAN
SPAIN
ITALY
GREECE
GEORGIA AZERBAIJAN
ARMENIA
UZBEKISTAN
TURKMENISTAN
KIRGISTAN
TAJIKISTAN
TURKEY
CYPRUS
ISRAEL
TUNISIA
SYRIA
JORDAN IRAQ
KUWAIT
IRAN
AFGHANISTAN
BHUTAN
CHINA
TAIWAN
OCCO
ALGERIA
LIBYA
EGYPT
PAKISTAN
NEPAL
BANGLADESH
BURMA
LAOS
VIETNAM
PHILIPPINES
SAUDI ARABIA
UAE
OMAN
INDIA
MALI
NIGER
ERITREA YEMEN
BURKINA FASO
GHANA BENIN
NIGERIA
CHAD
SUDAN
DJIBOUTI
THAILAND
CAMBODIA
TOGO CAMEROON
CENTRAL AFRICAN REPUBLIC
ETHIOPIA
SOMALIA
KENYA
MALAYSIA
CONGO
SEYCHELLES ○
TANZANIA
INDONESIA
ANGOLA
AUSTRALIA
NAMIBIA
SOUTH AFRICA
NEW ZEALAND

The myth of the unicorn is probably inspired by the **Arabian Oryx**. The last wild member of this species of antelope was shot in 1972. It has been sustained in captivity, including a herd raised in the USA. Although it has been re-introduced to Jordan, Israel and Saudi Arabia, poachers wrecked attempts at re-introduction in Oman.

The **Hirola or Hunter's Hartebeest** is critically endangered. It lives in southeastern Kenya. By 1995 the population had fallen to only 300, under the pressure of poaching and loss of habitat to domestic livestock.

WILD POPULATION OF ARABIAN ORYX

100 – 400	fewer than 200	none	approximately 500	886
1964	1969	1972	1998	2003

THREATENED UNGULATES
Number of species of ungulates classified as critically endangered, endangered or vulnerable *2000*

- 16 – 20
- 11 – 15
- 6 – 10
- 1 – 5
- none or no data

Number of ungulates classified as critically endangered

- 1
- 2
- 3

ELEPHANTS AND RHINOS

The elephant family comprises two species: the Indian elephant (*Elephas maximus*), weighing about 5.5 tonnes, and the African elephant (*Loxodonta africana*) weighing up to 7.5 tons and standing between 10 and 12 feet (3–4 m) at the shoulder. Both species live in habitats ranging from thick jungle to savanna. They form small family groups led by the eldest females, and where food is plentiful groups join to create larger herds. Most bulls live in bachelor herds apart from the cows. Elephants migrate seasonally, according to the availability of food and water. They spend many hours eating and may consume 500 lbs (225 kg) of grasses and other vegetation in a day.

For many centuries the Indian elephant has been used as both a ceremonial and draft animal. Elephants have been crucial to Southeast Asian logging operations, for example. African elephants are also used as working animals, but not as extensively.

Elephants are in great danger from habitat destruction and human exploitation. Both Indian and African elephants are classified as endangered; the African elephant suffers in particular from poaching for the ivory trade. Although conservation measures have been taken, including patrols to protect against poachers, and the creation of large reserves, these can lead to further problems. In good conditions, elephant populations can increase at a rate of 5 percent a year which leads to overpopulation and may make culling necessary. Corridor areas are vital to protect major migratory routes and to prevent herds from becoming isolated.

Rhinoceroses have one or two horns on the upper surface of the snout, composed of keratin, a fibrous protein found in hair. The Indian rhinoceros (*R. unicornis*) is the largest of the family, at about 14 feet (4.3 m) long and weighing up to 5 tons. Most rhinoceroses are solitary inhabitants of savanna, scrub forest, or marsh, although the Sumatran rhino is now found only in deep forest. Rhinoceroses have poor eyesight but acute hearing and sense of smell. Despite their bulk, they are remarkably agile; the black rhino may attain a speed of about 30 mph (45 kmph), even in thick brush.

All but the white rhinoceros are listed as endangered in the Red Data Book. Despite protective laws, poaching continues to supply a thriving market, with rhinoceros horn and blood among the most highly-prized ingredients in traditional medicines: rhino horns can fetch as much as US $60,000 per kilogram.

Captive-breeding programs offer the only hope for maintaining some species until adequate protection can be provided in the wild.

The **Indian elephant** is more closely related to the extinct mammoth than to the African elephant.

Mammoths are members of an extinct genus of elephants. The woolly Northern, or Siberian, mammoth is by far the best-known of all mammoths. Famished after the end of the Ice Age (11,000 years ago) by a diet of low-nutrient mosses, and increasingly harried by human hunters, the big grazers dwindled to extinction. Siberian mammoths were sometimes trapped in ice crevasses. Their bodies became remarkably well preserved in the ice and attempts are now underway to collect viable DNA from these beasts in the hope of being able to resurrect the species.

The **Javan rhino** is the rarest of the rhino species, with fewer than 60 animals surviving in only two known locations: one in Indonesia and the other in Vietnam. Rhinos have been poached from these small populations in recent years and much more intensive protection is needed if this species is to survive.

NEPAL BHUTAN

BANGLADESH

BURMA

INDIA

VIETNAM

THAILAND LAOS

CAMBODIA

SRI LANKA

BRUNEI

MALAYSIA

INDONESIA

The **Indian rhino** is one of the two greatest success stories in rhino conservation (the other being the southern white rhino in South Africa). With strict protection from Indian and Nepalese wildlife authorities, Indian rhino numbers have recovered from under 200 in the early 20th century to over 2,500. Poaching has, however, remained high and the success of conservation efforts is precarious without continued and increased support from the governments in India and Nepal.

DISTRIBUTION OF ELEPHANTS AND RHINOS *2000*

Number of rhinos, where known

Indian elephant	
African elephant	
African elephant recently extinct	
no native elephants	

25	White rhino
25	Black rhino
	Sumatran rhino
	Indian rhino
	Javan rhino

BEARS

Bears are among the largest of the carnivores and belong to the family *Ursidae*. Nine species are recognized, including the lesser panda (sometimes classified as a raccoon), and there are numerous subspecies. Six species are listed as threatened. Insufficient data exist about the sun or honey bear but this species is also feared to be threatened.

Bears vary in size from the sun bear, weighing only 66 lbs (30 kg), to the Kodiak brown bear, which can weigh 1,540 lbs (700 kg). Their diet varies as well. Polar bears are particularly fond of seals, panda bears eat mainly bamboo, and sloth bears prefer insects. Most bears, of course, eat honey.

Bears tend to live solitary lives, pairing only to mate. They are strong swimmers and smaller species are agile climbers.

Bears are hunted as trophies, for their hides, for meat and also from fear. When their territory overlaps with cultivated land, they are perceived as pests. Poachers kill bears for body parts and trap them for the pet trade or for use as performing animals. Bear gallbladders are used in traditional Chinese medicine to cure liver disease, cancer and other ailments.

In many parts of the world bears' habitats have been eroded and their populations fragmented, leading to the threat of local extinction. Small, insular groups of bears can also become weakened by genetic depletion.

Sophisticated management of hunting and habitat protection has sustained bear species living in North America and the Arctic, although pollution and global warming are serious problems (see pages 36-37). Resources for conservation in Asia and South America are not as plentiful, however, and a growing human population demands more land, which inevitably threaten bears. The establishment of wildlife "corridors" between reserves allows bears from different populations to mate and mix genes. Captive-breeding programs also offer hope for endangered bears. Over 100 giant pandas are kept in the world's zoos, but captivity impedes their breeding success rate as well as their life span.

The **brown bear**, called "grizzly" in North America, once ranged over all the northern continents. It has been hunted near to extinction in Europe, where only isolated populations totalling 13,000 remain in mountain ranges. Attempts to reintroduce bears into the Pyrénées seem doomed.

VENEZUELA
COLOMBIA
ECUADOR
PERU
BRAZIL
BOLIVIA
ARGENTINA

The **spectacled bear** is found in South America, living in terrains ranging from desert to rain forest, but it thrives best in cloud forest at around 2,000 metres. Logging and mining activites, and the expansion of agricultural land, is threatening the bear's survival. It is also hunted for its meat and skin. Attempts at conservation are hampered by unstable political environments and by drug trafficking.

In 2005 there were around 1,500 **giant pandas** left in the wild in mountain bamboo forests in central China. The 50 state-run nature reserves shelter two-thirds of them. The rest face the threat of deforestation and poaching. Even in protected reserves pandas now face the threat of starvation, as bamboo goes through its cyclical process of flowering and dying back. New growth can take 10 years to reappear.

THREATENED PANDAS
Species of panda considered under threat *2000*

Lesser Panda

Giant Panda

The Baluchistan bear, a subspecies of the **Asiatic black bear**, is critically endangered.

POPULATION OF THREATENED BEARS
2000

22,000–27,000

18,250

10,000–25,000

15,000–20,000

1,000

data deficient

polar bear

spectacled bear

sloth bear

Asiatic black bear

giant panda

sun bear

THREATENED BEARS
Species of bear considered under threat *2000*

Spectacled (Andean) Bear

Asiatic Black Bear

Sun (Honey) Bear

Sloth Bear

RODENTS

There are over 2,000 species of rodent, making them the most diverse order of mammals. They are found above and below ground and in all parts of the world except for New Zealand and the Antarctic. Most rodents are small – the dormouse weighs less than an ounce (20 grams) – although there are exceptions, such as the capybara of South America, which grows to 110 lbs (50 kg).

Rodents are commonly seen as agricultural pests, carriers of disease such as bubonic plague and as a threat to biodiversity. The black rat and Norway rat are cited as key villains, travelling all over the world via ships, wrecking food stores and displacing native rodent species. In fact, rodents are ecologically valuable. Some, such as squirrels, help plants to reproduce by burying seeds. Burrowing rodents mix, fertilize and aerate soil. As prey, rodents provide essential food for predators.

Rodent populations tend to be larger than those of other groups of mammals and their breeding rates are very high, making them well-equipped as a species to recover from adverse weather and epidemics. Despite this advantage, sustained pressure on rodent populations can cause local extermination; for species with only a limited range this can result in extinction.

The greatest threat to rodents is the progressive loss of their natural habitat from urbanization, cultivation of crops, and grazing of domestic livestock. Throughout the 20th century the US government sponsored a program of poisoning and plowing to eliminate prairie dogs, which degrade cattle-grazing land. As a result, the black-footed ferret, which preyed on the prairie dogs, disappeared. Although still classified as extinct in the wild, black-footed ferrets have been reintroduced with some success from a captive-bred population.

Fur trapping is illegal in many places, but continues to threaten some rodent species. Rarity and value tend to go hand in hand, thus encouraging trapping of the few remaining animals.

A MARMOT ON THE BRINK
Number of Vancouver Island Marmots in the wild

235   1984
102   1997
71   1998
57   1999

Colony of Vancouver Island Marmots

Vancouver Island

CANADA

UNITED STATES OF AMERICA

MEXICO

GUATEMALA   HONDURAS

BAHAMAS

CUBA

JAMAICA   HAITI

DOMINICAN REPUBLIC

COSTA RICA

PANAMA

COLOMBIA

ECUADOR

VENEZUELA

ST VINCENT & THE GRENADINES

GUYANA

SURINAME

FRENCH GUIANA (Fr)

PERU

BRAZIL

BOLIVIA

PARAGUAY

CHILE

ARGENTINA

BELG.

FRAN

PORTUGAL   SPAIN

MOROCCO

MAURITA

SENEGAL

North American beavers dam rivers to create wetlands, providing habitat for a wide range of other animals. They were almost driven to extinction by fur trappers and land drainage in the early 20th century.

The population of the **short-tailed chinchilla** collapsed by 80% in the last decade of the 20th century due to depletion of its habitat in the mountains of South America, and illegal trapping for its valuable fur. It is now critically endangered.

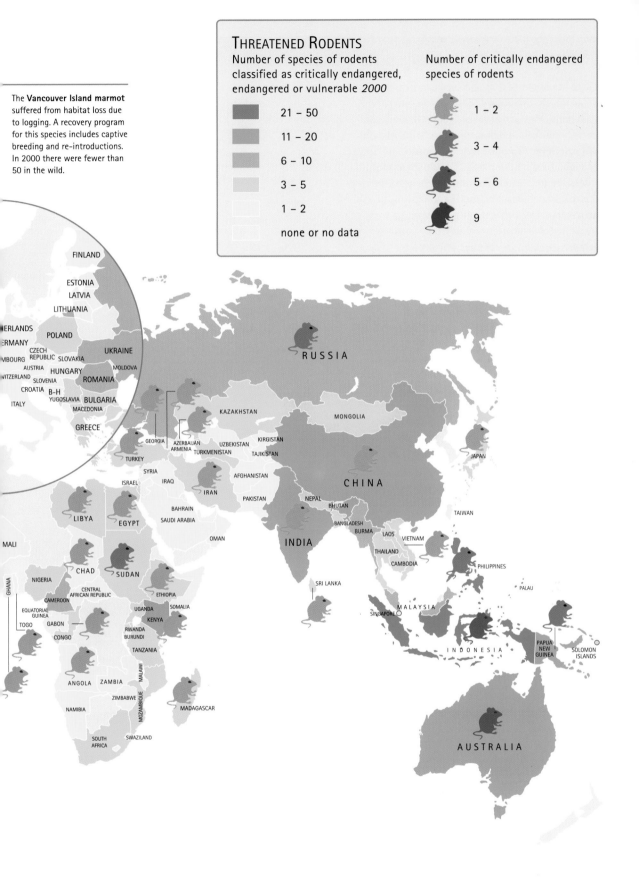

The **Vancouver Island marmot** suffered from habitat loss due to logging. A recovery program for this species includes captive breeding and re-introductions. In 2000 there were fewer than 50 in the wild.

THREATENED RODENTS

Number of species of rodents classified as critically endangered, endangered or vulnerable *2000*

- 21 – 50
- 11 – 20
- 6 – 10
- 3 – 5
- 1 – 2
- none or no data

Number of critically endangered species of rodents

- 1 – 2
- 3 – 4
- 5 – 6
- 9

BATS

There are about 900 species of bats, nearly a third of which are threatened. Bats are the only flying mammals. Most eat insects, although some eat nectar and fruit, helping to pollinate plants and disperse seeds. Vampire bats in Central and South America feed on the blood of large mammals.

Bats are nocturnal, avoiding the heat of the day, the risk of dehydration and the attentions of predators. They navigate at night using a form of sonar or echo-location. By day they roost in trees and caves, often in colonies of over a million bats. In urban areas they roost in buildings.

Bats are distributed over temperate and tropical regions but are most abundant near the equator. Those that spend the summer in temperate regions either hibernate or migrate towards the equator in winter. Most produce only one offspring each year, so bat populations tend to recover slowly from catastrophic events.

Bats bring several benefits to humans. Their droppings contain nitrogen and phosphorus and are collected for use as fertilizer. They also help to control populations of insects that are pests of crops and carry diseases. A single bat can kill 20,000 insects in one night. In contrast, they have only a few drawbacks for humans. Some commercial fruit farmers have to use nets to protect their crops from bats, and vampire bats can transmit diseases including rabies to their animal hosts.

Humans, on the other hand, threaten the survival of bats in many ways. Some bats, such as the large flying foxes of Southeast Asia, are hunted for food. Species such as Mexican fishing bats have became locally extinct following the introduction by humans of cats and rats to their island habitats. Mining, waste disposal and irresponsible tourism threaten the caves where bats roost.

Bats have suffered grievously from the loss of their natural habitat to agriculture and forestry. A vicious cycle ensues. The decline of bats in agricultural areas causes farmers to use more chemicals to control insect pests, which risks poisoning the few remaining bats.

The endangered **lesser long-nosed bat** is one of the few bat pollinators in the southwestern USA, and is vital to the survival of agaves and giant cacti in the Sonoran Desert.

CANADA

UNITED STATES OF AMERICA

PORTUGAL

MOROCCO

BAHAMAS

CUBA

MEXICO

BELIZE JAMAICA
GUATEMALA HONDURAS
EL SALVADOR

US VIRGIN
ISLANDS
MONTSERRAT
PUERTO
RICO
DOMINICA

GUADELOUPE

SENEGAL

NICARAGUA

ARUBA NETHERLANDS ANTILLES

GUINEA
SIERRA LEONE
LIBERIA

COSTA RICA

PANAMA

VENEZUELA GUYANA
SURINAME
FRENCH GUIANA (Fr)

COLOMBIA

ECUADOR

BRAZIL

PERU

BOLIVIA

PARAGUAY

CHILE

URUGUAY

ARGENTINA

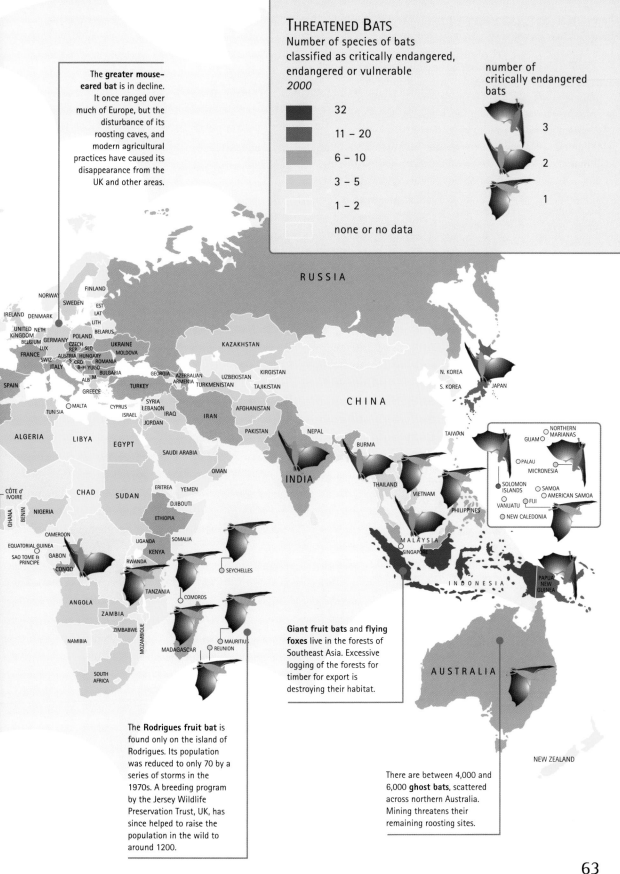

THREATENED BATS
Number of species of bats classified as critically endangered, endangered or vulnerable
2000

32
11 – 20
6 – 10
3 – 5
1 – 2
none or no data

number of critically endangered bats
3
2
1

The **greater mouse-eared bat** is in decline. It once ranged over much of Europe, but the disturbance of its roosting caves, and modern agricultural practices have caused its disappearance from the UK and other areas.

Giant fruit bats and **flying foxes** live in the forests of Southeast Asia. Excessive logging of the forests for timber for export is destroying their habitat.

The **Rodrigues fruit bat** is found only on the island of Rodrigues. Its population was reduced to only 70 by a series of storms in the 1970s. A breeding program by the Jersey Wildlife Preservation Trust, UK, has since helped to raise the population in the wild to around 1200.

There are between 4,000 and 6,000 **ghost bats**, scattered across northern Australia. Mining threatens their remaining roosting sites.

DOLPHINS AND WHALES

Dolphins, whales and porpoises are all classified as *Cetacea*. Some dolphins are fish, but most are aquatic mammals. The 44 species of mammalian dolphins include pilot and killer whales, and river dolphins living in South America and Asia. Dolphins usually live in groups and mainly eat fish. They are highly intelligent, and use sounds and ultrasonic pulses to communicate.

Dolphins are at risk from drowning after becoming ensnared in fishing nets. Those that live in rivers and estuaries are also adversely affected by chemical pollution and silting, and having to compete for food with humans. Their limited distribution makes them particularly vulnerable.

All whales (including the seven species of porpoise) are mammals. They must come to the water's surface to breathe through blowholes. Some whales (including the sperm, bottle-nosed, beaked and beluga) have teeth and eat fish. Others (including the gray, right, humpback and blue) strain plankton and krill from the water, using a dense fringe of blade-shaped horny plates ("baleen") in their mouths. Some whales are social, traveling in groups. They use a range of underwater sounds: barks, whistles, screams, and moans, for communication, and high-intensity clicks for navigation and to identify food sources.

Dead whales yield several products of commercial value, including meat, oil, whalebone, and ambergris which is used in perfume. Hundreds of years of whaling by increasingly effective methods has led to the near-extinction of several species, in particular the blue whale. The International Whaling Commission, set up in 1946, has attempted to combat this threat – both to whales and to the livelihood of the whalers. First it introduced quotas to give whale populations an opportunity to re-establish themselves. Then, in 1983, it introduced a temporary moratorium on commercial whaling, to take effect by 1986. Although this has not been entirely successful, it has reduced the number of whales killed, and some species, such as gray and humpback whales, are showing signs of recovery.

For some communities, whaling provides an important part of their diet, and plays a key role in their economy and culture. These are exempt

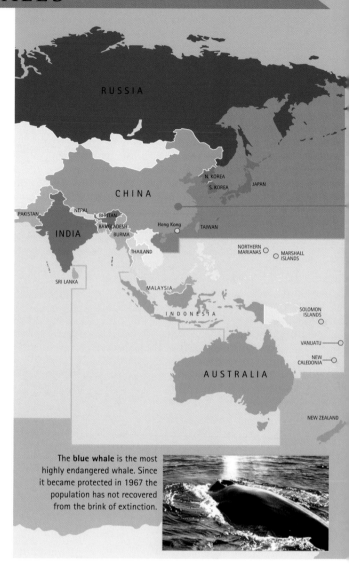

The **blue whale** is the most highly endangered whale. Since it became protected in 1967 the population has not recovered from the brink of extinction.

from the ban on commercial whaling. People from Greenland hunt fin and minke whales, those in Siberia hunt gray whales. In Alaska bowhead, and occasionally gray, whales are caught.

Whales are affected by human development, as their breeding and calving areas are often in shallow coastal waters. But tourism, in the form of "whale watching", now helps support the economies of towns and villages that once relied on income from hunting whales. It also helps to promote public understanding and appreciation of whales, which may influence governments' inclination to continue to protect them.

The **Chinese Lake Dolphin** (the "Beiji") is critically endangered, with estimates of perhaps 100 animals left in the wild, and only 2 in captivity. Its plight has been caused by deteriorating water quality in its habitat, the Yangtze River.

Noise from ice-breakers may damage the hearing of **beluga whales** and mask their communication, potentially affecting breeding.

The Gulf of California **Harbour Porpoise** is critically endangered.

A **whale sanctuary** was established by the IWC in 1994, permanently banning whaling in the waters around the Antarctic.

THREATENED DOLPHINS AND WHALES

Number of species of cetacea classified as critically endangered, endangered and vulnerable *2000*

Inland and territorial waters

- 9 – 10
- 7 – 8
- 5 – 6
- 3 – 4
- 1 – 2
- none or no data

International waters

- 11 – 16
- 6 – 10
- 1 – 5

GREAT WHALE POPULATIONS

Total populations of the larger species of whales *2000*

Minke whale 935,000

Fin whale 47,300

Gray whale 26,300

Humpback whale 15,500

Blue whale 400–1,400

Bowhead whale 7,500

Pilot whale 780,000

GREENLAND
JAN MAYEN
SVALBARD
ICELAND
FAEROE ISLANDS
SWEDEN FINLAND
NORWAY
EST LAT LITH
DENMARK
RUSSIA
IRELAND UNITED KINGDOM
NETH GERMANY POLAND
BELGIUM
FRANCE ITALY UKRAINE
MOLDOVA
ROMANIA
PORTUGAL SPAIN
BULG GEORGIA
TURKEY
CANADA
TUNISIA
MOROCCO
IRAQ
BERMUDA
UAE
UNITED STATES OF AMERICA
MEXICO
CUBA
BAHAMAS
DOMINICAN REPUBLIC
MAURITANIA
CAPE VERDE
SENEGAL
ERITREA
NETHERLANDS ANTILLES
ST LUCIA
ST VINCENT
NICARAGUA
COSTA RICA
PANAMA
VENEZUELA
GUYANA
SURINAME
LIBERIA
COLOMBIA
ECUADOR
CONGO
DEMOCRATIC REPUBLIC OF CONGO
KENYA
PERU
BRAZIL
ST HELENA
TANZANIA
BOLIVIA
ANGOLA
SAMOA
AMERICAN SAMOA
FRENCH POLYNESIA
FIJI
TONGA
COOK ISLAND
NAMIBIA
MOZAMBIQUE
MADAGASCAR
CHILE
SOUTH AFRICA
ARGENTINA
URUGUAY
FALKLAND ISLANDS (UK)

REPTILES AND AMPHIBIANS

Reptiles are air-breathing vertebrates that have internal fertilization and scaly bodies. They include snakes, lizards, turtles, crocodiles and alligators.

The skins of lizards, crocodiles and snakes are used to make leather goods such as luggage, handbags and shoes. This has led to the virtual extinction of several species of crocodile and to a severe reduction in the populations of large lizards, snakes, and turtles.

Vertebrates such as frogs, toads and salamanders that are able to exploit both water and land habitats are known as amphibians (from the Greek for "living a double life"). Despite this description, however, some species are permanent land dwellers, while others are completely aquatic. Amphibians absorb oxygen through their skin, which is kept moist by mucus-secreting glands.

The Global Amphibian Assessment, published in 2005, indicated that almost a third of amphibian species were threatened with extinction. Because of their absorbent skins, amphibians are susceptible to water pollution, even at low concentrations, or in protected areas some distance from the source of pollution. They are therefore considered one of the best indicators of pollution in the environment.

Because amphibians rely on moisture, they are also affected by changes in weather patterns. In the Americas, the Caribbean and Australia frog numbers have plummeted in recent years, largely because of the fungus chytrid, which attacks keratin in their skin, producing toxins and preventing them from using their skins to breathe. Scientists now think that it may be linked to drought, which is becoming increasingly frequent because of recent climate change.

Since the early 1990s environmentally conscious Australians have been reintroducing tadpoles into ponds and streams in an attempt to bolster flagging populations. This not only spreads disease, but introduces alien genes or even alien species that displace native frogs. Exotic frog species are also being introduced accidentally, imported in crates of fruit, vegetables, and flowers.

Deformities in frogs around the North American Great Lakes are thought to be due to pollution. Organochlorines, for example, disrupt frogs' endocrine (hormone) systems.

The **marine iguana** is only found on the Galapagos Islands and is therefore vulnerable to local pollution and the destruction of its habitat.

CANADA

UNITED STATES OF AMERICA
1

MEXICO

○ BERMUDA

BAHAMAS
CUBA   TURKS
            & CAICOS
CAYMAN   DOMINICAN
ISLANDS ○   REP.
BELIZE JAMAICA   HAITI
GUATEMALA HONDURAS   PUERTO
EL SALVADOR   RICO
NICARAGUA
COSTA RICA
PANAMA

VIRGIN ISLANDS (USA)
1
VIRGIN ISLANDS (UK)
ANTIGUA & BARBUDA
ST KITTS NEVIS
GUADELOUPE
DOMINICA
MARTINIQUE
ARUBA   NETH.   ST LUCIA
(NETH.) ANTILLES BARBADOS
         GRENADA
         TRINIDAD & TOBAGO
VENEZUELA   GUYANA
             SURINAME
COLOMBIA   FRENCH GUIANA (Fr)
1
2

GALAPAGOS
ISLANDS
1
ECUADOR

PERU   BRAZIL

FRENCH   BOLIVIA
POLYNESIA
○
                PARAGUAY

CHILE   URUGUAY
        ARGENTINA

WESTER
SAHAR
CAPE VERDE ○   MAURITAN
1   SENEGAL
                GAMBIA
                GUINEA-BISSAU
                        GUIN
                SIERRA LEONE
                        LIBER

Copyright © Myriad Editions Limited

THREATENED AMPHIBIANS

Number of species of amphibians classified as critically endangered, endangered or vulnerable *2004*

- more than 100
- 51 – 100
- 11 – 50
- 1 – 10
- none or no data

The **Asian three-striped box turtle** is killed for use in Chinese medicine. Believed to cure cancer, Its population has declined drastically in recent years.

THREATENED REPTILES

Number of species of reptiles classified as critically endangered, endangered or vulnerable *2004*

- more than 20
- 11 – 20
- 6 – 10
- 1 – 5
- none or no data

number of species of reptile known to have become extinct

INVERTEBRATES

Invertebrates are animals that lack backbones. They comprise over 90 percent of animal species. Some invertebrates are soft-bodied but many have a hard outer skeleton that provides protection and anchorage for muscles; these animals are called "arthropods". The three groups of arthropods are *chelicerates* (spiders, scorpions and mites), *crustaceans* (crabs and shrimps) and *uniramians* (insects and centipedes).

The range of size and habitat of invertebrates is staggering. Some plankton measure less than two-hundredths of an inch (0.5 mm), while giant squid can grow up to 33 feet (10 metres) long. Crustaceans have been found over 2.5 miles (4 km) under the sea and spiders have been seen on Mount Everest. The practical difficulties in catching and inspecting smaller invertebrates means that the number of species can only be estimated. Some experts suggest that the number of species of insects alone is over 10 million and more are being discovered every year in remote areas of rainforest.

As new invertebrates are identified, other species are being added to the IUCN Red List. Identifying a species under threat requires money and effort. This map, together with others in the atlas, reveals a strong correlation between the number of species of invertebrates recognized as under threat in a country and the investment put into investigating them.

Invertebrates play a crucial role in many ecosystems. Other animals often rely on them for food. The plankton of the oceans support higher forms of life, including whales. Invertebrates can help in other ways too – insects pollinate flowering plants, and worms mix and aerate soil.

Some invertebrates, such as butterflies, capture the public imagination, but most are perceived of as distasteful or at least too numerous to warrant concern for their conservation. Invertebrates with restricted habitats or limited mobility are at risk both from human development and from climate change, which could, for example, eliminate a species that occurs only on a single mountain.

Monarch butterflies migrate to Mexico for the winter from as far away as Canada. Almost all over-wintering Monarchs are concentrated in just eight groves of trees, with as many as 100,000 huddling together on a single tree for warmth. Disturbance by loggers can cause Monarchs to scatter on arrival in the autumn, jeopardizing their ability to mate the following spring. Climate change will bring more rain to these groves and the ice that forms kills Monarchs.

The **Harlequin ladybird** was introduced from Asia to North America and Europe to control aphids. It has devastated native ladybirds by predation and competition for food.

THREATENED INVERTEBRATES

Number of species of invertebrate classified as critically endangered, endangered or vulnerable *2004*

- more than 50
- 21 – 50
- 11 – 20
- 6 – 10
- 1 – 5
- none or no data
- over 100 threatened invertebrates

THREATENED CRUSTACEANS

Number of species in each IUCN Red List category *2004*

- 56 critically endangered
- 79 endangered
- 294 vulnerable

101

283

FISH

Fish are found in rivers, lakes and oceans all over the world, and range in size from a tiny goby, half an inch (12.5 mm) in length, to the 50-foot (15-metre) whale shark. Oceanic fish range over large areas, and similar species occur around the world. Estuary and freshwater fish, however, tend to be isolated from neighbouring populations and have developed greater diversity as they adapt to their environment.

Fish congregate in schools to feed, breed and minimize the risk (to each individual) from predators. They lay eggs that hatch into larvae and develop into adult fish. Larvae and adult fish have different needs, and often live far apart. Oceanic fish may, for example, have coastal or freshwater spawning grounds.

Humans have fished the seas since prehistoric times. Most of the modern global catch comprises salt-water fish. Countries have control over fisheries in an "exclusive economic zone" up to 200 miles (320 km) from their coasts – or to the midpoint between opposing coasts. Despite this and other measures to define fishing quotas, most commercial fisheries are seriously depleted.

Freshwater fish, which represent only 6 percent of all fish caught, tend to be eaten locally, often providing crucial dietary protein in rural societies. Because freshwater species occur in limited areas, they are especially vulnerable to over-fishing and ecological damage. Dams and channels fragment habitats. Effluent and agricultural chemicals pollute them. Water abstraction sucks rivers dry.

Aquaculture (fish farming) accounts for about one-third of fish eaten around the world. Although Asia is responsible for about 90 percent of production, the industry is growing rapidly in Central and South America and in Africa.

Although aquaculture is hailed by some as a solution to the depletion of wild fish stocks, carnivorous fish such as salmon and shrimp may require 2 to 4 kilograms of fish protein, derived from captured wild fish, for every kilogram produced. In addition, the waste emitted by unregulated enterprises can be highly damaging to fragile coastal ecosystems such as mangroves. Human health may also suffer from contaminants passed down in fish feed.

In 1997 the World Wide Fund for Nature and Unilever founded the Marine Stewardship Council (MSC), which established a set of principles and criteria of good fishing management. In Alaska, where overfishing had reduced salmon harvests to about 25 million fish in 1959, habitat protection has allowed stocks to recover sufficiently to enable a commercial salmon catch of 168 million fish in 2004.

Lake Victoria, the largest tropical lake in the world, used to hold over 300 species of small cichlid fish. In 1954 Nile perch were introduced to increase the size of the fishing catch. They demolished the cichlids, causing the extinction of hundreds of species. Algae, on which cichlids feed, now grow unchecked and strip oxygen from the water, jeopardizing the whole lake ecosystem.

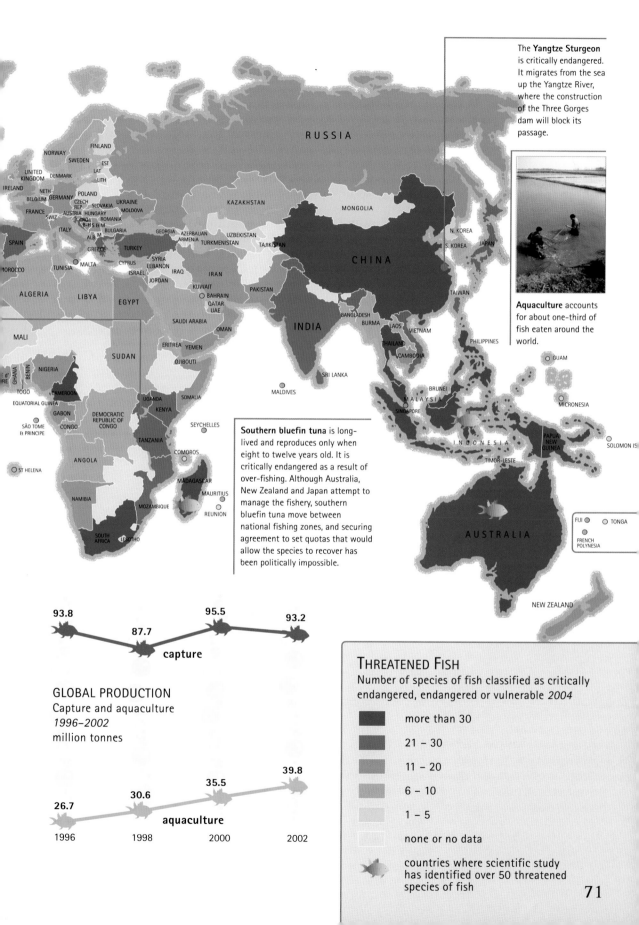

The **Yangtze Sturgeon** is critically endangered. It migrates from the sea up the Yangtze River, where the construction of the Three Gorges dam will block its passage.

Aquaculture accounts for about one-third of fish eaten around the world.

Southern bluefin tuna is long-lived and reproduces only when eight to twelve years old. It is critically endangered as a result of over-fishing. Although Australia, New Zealand and Japan attempt to manage the fishery, southern bluefin tuna move between national fishing zones, and securing agreement to set quotas that would allow the species to recover has been politically impossible.

93.8   87.7   95.5   93.2
capture

GLOBAL PRODUCTION
Capture and aquaculture
1996–2002
million tonnes

26.7   30.6   35.5   39.8
aquaculture

1996   1998   2000   2002

THREATENED FISH
Number of species of fish classified as critically endangered, endangered or vulnerable *2004*

- more than 30
- 21 – 30
- 11 – 20
- 6 – 10
- 1 – 5
- none or no data
- countries where scientific study has identified over 50 threatened species of fish

71

PLANTS

Plants are vital to the survival of all other life forms on earth, forming the basis of most animal food chains, including that of humans. Plants harness the sun's energy to produce their own food through the process of photosynthesis. They absorb carbon dioxide and release oxygen, helping to maintain a healthy atmosphere.

The plant kingdom is incredibly diverse, ranging from simple mosses to complex flowering plants and the 300-foot (100-meter) high redwood tree. There are between 275,000 and 300,000 species of vascular plants (ferns, conifers and flowering plants), around 34,000 of which are threatened with extinction (see right).

Humans often carry plants and their seeds around the world, sometimes intentionally to grow for food and for decoration, sometimes inadvertently. Predators and diseases that afflict native plants are often not well adapted to attack these introduced, "exotic", plant species. As a result some exotic species become "invasive", competing with and displacing native species of plants. Exotic species may also interbreed with native plants, giving rise to hybrids. Plants endemic to a small area of land or an island are particularly at risk. Native plants on islands such as Hawaii and St. Helena, for example, have been devastated by invasive species.

Habitat destruction is an even greater threat to plant diversity. Human settlement and intensive farming continue to encroach on natural areas, threatening plants such as the Alabama canebrake pitcher-plant, which is now critically endangered following drainage of over 50 percent of the wetlands of Alabama. Unsustainable logging in forests around the world also threatens the survival of many endemic populations of plants (see pages 22-25), just as the world is waking up to the vital medicinal qualities of many species.

The **lady's slipper orchid** grows on limestone soils across the northern hemisphere. Because of its beauty it is prized by plant collectors, and has therefore always been rare. The remaining plants suffer from habitat destruction by logging and agriculture.

endangered/extinct
31

indeterminate
4,070

endangered
6,522

rare
14,505

vulnerable
7,951

EXTENT OF THE THREAT
Number of species of plant in each IUCN Red List category *1997*

total
33,418 species

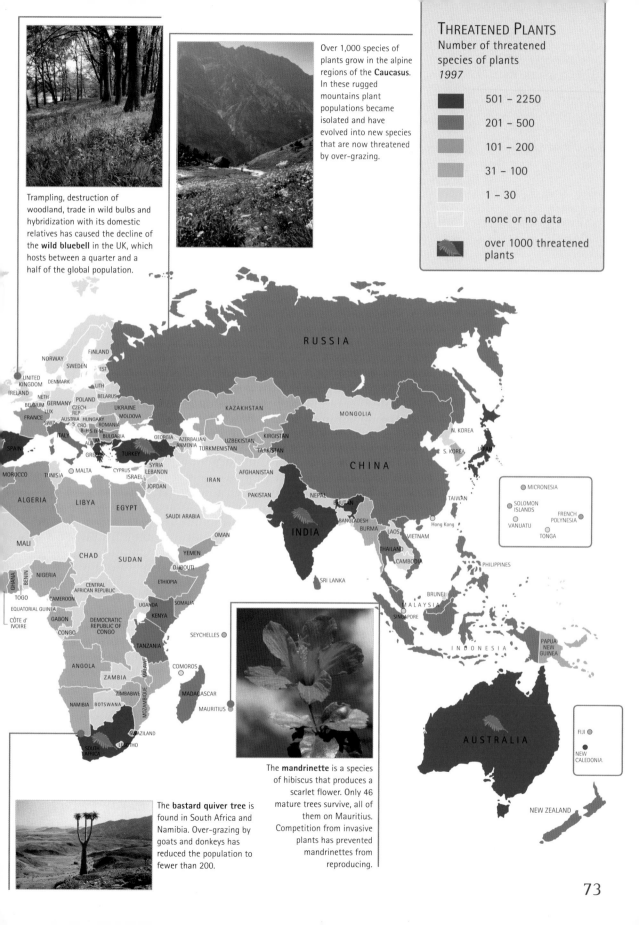

Trampling, destruction of woodland, trade in wild bulbs and hybridization with its domestic relatives has caused the decline of the **wild bluebell** in the UK, which hosts between a quarter and a half of the global population.

Over 1,000 species of plants grow in the alpine regions of the **Caucasus**. In these rugged mountains plant populations became isolated and have evolved into new species that are now threatened by over-grazing.

THREATENED PLANTS
Number of threatened species of plants
1997

- 501 – 2250
- 201 – 500
- 101 – 200
- 31 – 100
- 1 – 30
- none or no data
- over 1000 threatened plants

The **bastard quiver tree** is found in South Africa and Namibia. Over-grazing by goats and donkeys has reduced the population to fewer than 200.

The **mandrinette** is a species of hibiscus that produces a scarlet flower. Only 46 mature trees survive, all of them on Mauritius. Competition from invasive plants has prevented mandrinettes from reproducing.

ENDANGERED BIRDS

5

"The sedge is wither'd from the lake,
And no birds sing."

— John Keats,
"La Belle Dame Sans Merci" (1817)

BIRDS

Birds are warm-blooded vertebrates that have developed hollow bones, wings and feathers that enable most, but not all, to fly. Most birds are omnivores, eating insects, reptiles, amphibians, mammals, fish and other birds, as well as vegetable matter such as seeds.

In 2005, an estimated 12 percent (over 1,200) of all known species of bird were considered under threat.

The greatest threat to birds is human destruction of their habitat through logging, commercial development and intensive agriculture, and the introduction of new predators, competitors and diseases. Even domestic cats, if allowed to roam free, can kill hundreds of small birds each year. Uncontrolled hunting and trapping threatens many species of birds. The imperial woodpecker, which once lived in upland forest in north eastern Mexico, was one of many species driven to extinction in the 20th century by deforestation and hunting. Migratory birds are especially vulnerable to trapping and shooting.

Intensive agriculture also threatens farmland birds, especially in North America and Europe. Winter sowing produces crops too dense for birds to nest in, and the frequent cutting of summer grass for silage destroys their nest sites. Skylark populations have decreased sharply in western Europe, but in eastern Europe, where intensive methods are not yet widespread, the bird's populations tend to be more stable.

Climate change worldwide affects the fragile balance between birds and their food supply. Plants are flowering earlier in the spring, and changes to vegetation are altering the abundance of insects, worms and other creatures. This is likely to have a significant impact on the breeding and migratory patterns of birds.

In Southeast Asia, Africa and South America deforestation is occurring at a rapid rate (see pages 42-43), and at each review more tropical rainforest birds are classified as threatened. Rainforest species, such as the Indonesian caerulean paradise-flycatcher, are most at risk from unsustainable logging and forest clearance for agriculture and exotic timber plantations.

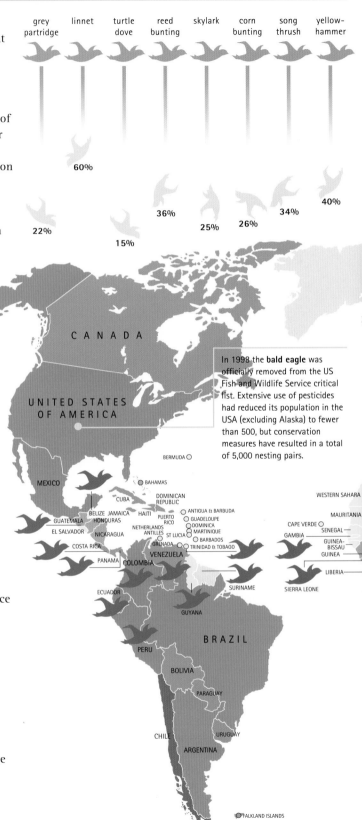

grey partridge — 60%

linnet

turtle dove — 15%

reed bunting — 36%

skylark — 25%

corn bunting — 26%

song thrush — 34%

yellow-hammer — 40%

22%

In 1998 the **bald eagle** was officially removed from the US Fish and Wildlife Service critical list. Extensive use of pesticides had reduced its population in the USA (excluding Alaska) to fewer than 500, but conservation measures have resulted in a total of 5,000 nesting pairs.

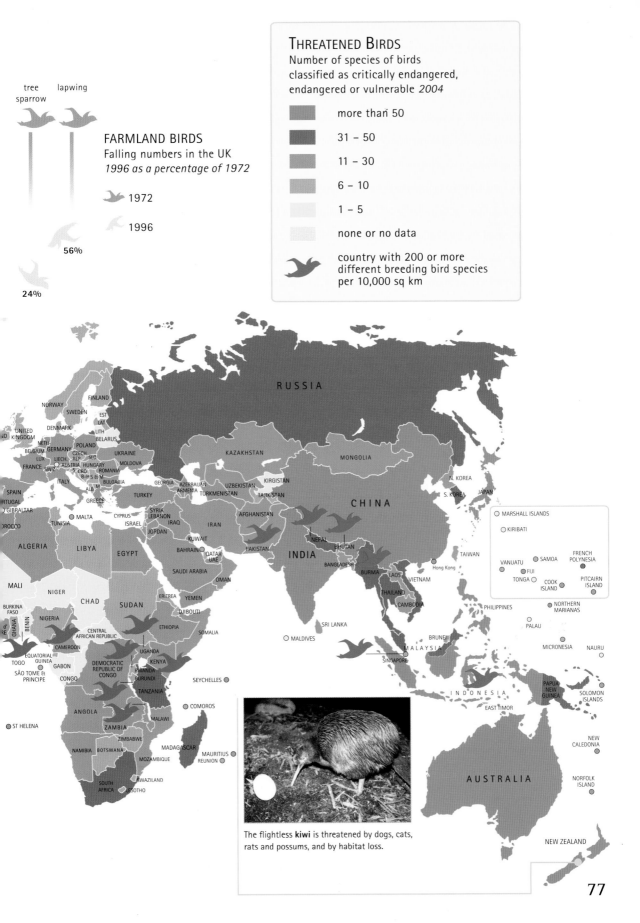

FARMLAND BIRDS
Falling numbers in the UK
1996 as a percentage of 1972

tree sparrow lapwing

1972

1996

56%

24%

THREATENED BIRDS
Number of species of birds
classified as critically endangered,
endangered or vulnerable *2004*

more than 50

31 – 50

11 – 30

6 – 10

1 – 5

none or no data

country with 200 or more
different breeding bird species
per 10,000 sq km

The flightless **kiwi** is threatened by dogs, cats,
rats and possums, and by habitat loss.

77

BIRDS OF PREY

Birds of prey include owls, and raptors such as hawks, eagles, vultures, and falcons. All birds of prey have talons for seizing their quarry, and curved beaks for tearing its flesh. They have good vision and hearing, but often a poor sense of smell. Raptors hunt during the day, and owls are nocturnal. Raptors eat other birds, mammals and carrion. Some, such as the bald eagle, can pluck fish from water. They are all skillful fliers and larger species have long, broad wings for soaring.

Many birds of prey have suffered from loss of habitat. Each breeding pair requires a large territory, which is often difficult to protect from development. Many of the chemicals used in farming are toxic to birds of prey. For example, the organochlorine pesticide DDT causes the shells of eagles' eggs to thin, making them prone to break. Prohibition of the use of such pesticides in developed countries has helped protect birds of prey, but developing countries often cannot afford the less damaging but more expensive alternatives. Birds such as the Steller's sea eagle, which feed on animals that have been shot, often suffer from lead poisoning as a result. Other birds of prey are killed for sport and food, and captured for falconry – all of which further depletes the populations of some species.

Habitat protection plays a critical role in the conservation of birds of prey. Control of poaching is important too. In many countries it is illegal to hunt birds of prey, steal their eggs or disturb their nests. Captive breeding and rehabilitation centers for injured birds can significantly help species at risk of extinction.

The **California condor** population fell below 100 in 1940 because of hunting and lead poisoning. In 1987 the remaining nine birds were captured for a breeding program at Los Angeles Zoo and at the San Diego Wild Animal Park. This has held the species back from the brink of extinction and by 2000 there were 57 reintroduced California condors living in the wild, with 98 in captivity.

CALIFORNIAN CONDOR IN CRISIS
Number of individual birds in the wild

fewer than 100

50 – 60

57

0

1940   1967   1987   2000

DECLINE OF ASIAN WHITE-BACKED VULTURE
Breeding population in Keoladeo National Park, near Bharatpur, India

UNITED STATES OF AMERICA

MEXICO

CUBA

HAITI

DOMINICAN REPUBLIC

COLOMBIA

ECUADOR

PERU

BOLIVIA

BRAZIL

PARAGUAY

URUGUAY

ARGENTINA

FRANC

PORTUGAL   SPAIN

GIBRALTAR

ALGERIA

MOROCCO

WESTERN SAHARA

MAURITANIA

SENEGAL
GAMBIA
GUINEA-BISSAU
GUINEA
SIERRA LEONE
LIBERIA

79

THREATENED BIRDS OF PREY

Number of species of birds of prey classified as critically endangered, endangered or vulnerable *2000*

- 7 or more
- 5 – 6
- 3 – 4
- 1 – 2
- none or no data

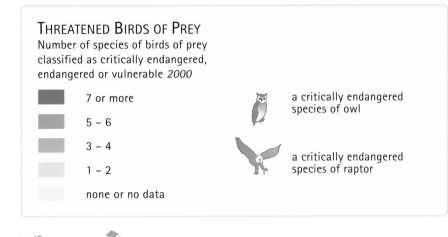 a critically endangered species of owl

a critically endangered species of raptor

FINLAND
SWEDEN
ESTONIA
LATVIA
LITHUANIA
GERMANY
POLAND
BELARUS
CZECH REPUBLIC
SLOVAKIA
UKRAINE
AUSTRIA
HUNGARY
MOLDOVA
VITZERLAND
SLOVENIA
ROMANIA
ITALY
B-H
S & M
BULGARIA
ALBANIA
MACEDONIA
GREECE
MALTA
TUNISIA
TURKEY
CYPRUS
SYRIA
LEBANON
ISRAEL
PALESTINE
JORDAN
IRAQ
KUWAIT
ALGERIA
LIBYA
EGYPT
BAHRAIN
QATAR
UAE
SAUDI ARABIA
OMAN
MALI
NIGER
CHAD
SUDAN
ERITREA
YEMEN
DJIBOUTI
3URKINA FASO
GHANA
BENIN
NIGERIA
ETHIOPIA
TE d'
DIRE
TOGO
CAMEROON
EQUATORIAL GUINEA
CENTRAL AFRICAN REPUBLIC
SOMALIA
GABON
CONGO
UGANDA
KENYA
RWANDA
BURUNDI
TANZANIA
SEYCHELLES
ANGOLA
ZAMBIA
MALAWI
COMOROS
MAYOTTE
ZIMBABWE
MOZAMBIQUE
NAMIBIA
BOTSWANA
MADAGASCAR
MAURITIUS
REUNION
SOUTH AFRICA
SWAZILAND
LESOTHO

RUSSIA
KAZAKHSTAN
MONGOLIA
N. KOREA
S. KOREA
JAPAN
GEORGIA
AZERBAIJAN
ARMENIA
UZBEKISTAN
KIRGISTAN
TURKMENISTAN
TAJIKISTAN
CHINA
IRAN
AFGHANISTAN
PAKISTAN
NEPAL
BHUTAN
TAIWAN
Hong Kong
BANGLADESH
BURMA
INDIA
LAOS
THAILAND
VIETNAM
CAMBODIA
PHILIPPINES
MALDIVES
BRUNEI
MALAYSIA
SINGAPORE
KIRITINATI
INDONESIA
PAPUA NEW GUINEA
SOLOMON ISLANDS
AUSTRALIA

The **Great Philippine eagle**, which produces a single chick every two years, is vulnerable to clearance of its rain-forest habitat for logging and farming. No more than 300 survive, almost all on the island of Mindanao.

353 nests
1987–88

150 nests
1996–97

25 nests
1997–98

20 nests
1998–99

0 nests
1999–2000

The **white-backed** and **long-billed vultures**, once seen circling in flocks of 2,000 in the Indian subcontinent, are now nearing extinction, killed off by consuming the carcasses of cattle that had been treated for arthritis with diclofenac. This causes kidney failure in the vultures and leads to death within 30 days. The birds performed the important function of consuming the dead bodies of livestock and, for those of the Parsee faith, of humans. This role is increasingly being filled by feral dogs, leading to an alarming increase in rabies.

PARROTS AND COCKATOOS

There are over 300 species of parrot, including lorikeets, cockatoos and parakeets. As many as 95 of them, or 28 percent, are threatened – the highest proportion of any of the major bird families.

Parrots come in a variety of sizes and shapes. The pygmy parrot can be less than 3 inches (10 cm) long, while some macaws grow to over 3 feet (1 metre) in length. Most are brightly coloured. Parrots have strong, hooked beaks, which they use for breaking open nuts. Many plants, such as the oil palm, rely on parrots to disperse their seeds. A few parrots are predatory. For example, the New Zealand kea is known to attack sheep.

Most parrots live in tropical forests, nesting in tree holes. They are not built for flying long distances, which means that species are often restricted to isolated islands, making them especially vulnerable. In the West Indies at least 16 species are known to have been exterminated by European explorers, and the Puerto Rican parrot is critically endangered (see right).

Parrots, particularly the African Gray and Amazon, are excellent mimics. This ability, along with their friendly nature and lively plumage, make them popular in zoos and also as pets, with most demand coming from Europe and Japan. Some countries, such as Mexico and Australia, forbid the export of parrots in order to conserve wild populations. Despite such efforts, the legal and illegal trade in parrots is huge, threatening the viability of wild populations. Poaching alone affects 39 species and is a greater cause of mortality than natural causes.

Parrots are hunted for food, and some seed-eating parrots are hunted by farmers because they are considered to be pests. Introduced predators, such as cats, are a hazard and imported birds can displace native parrot species or introduce avian diseases.

The greatest threat to most parrot species is loss of habitat, from fire, logging and human settlement. The Species Survival Commission's conservation action plan for parrots presents techniques for their conservation in the face of habitat destruction and illegal hunting. Scarce resources in the face of competing economic interests may frustrate its effective adoption.

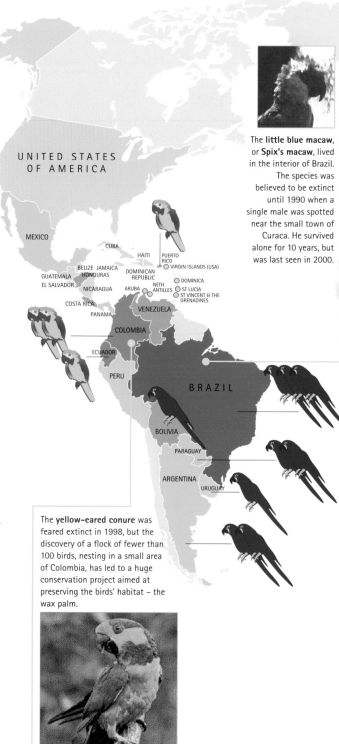

The **little blue macaw**, or **Spix's macaw**, lived in the interior of Brazil. The species was believed to be extinct until 1990 when a single male was spotted near the small town of Curaca. He survived alone for 10 years, but was last seen in 2000.

The **yellow-eared conure** was feared extinct in 1998, but the discovery of a flock of fewer than 100 birds, nesting in a small area of Colombia, has led to a huge conservation project aimed at preserving the birds' habitat – the wax palm.

The **hyacinth macaw**, is the largest parrot in the world, but its size is no protection. It is threatened by the trade in exotic species and the destruction of its nesting habitat.

PUERTO RICAN AMAZON PARROT
Number of parrots

in the wild

in captivity

In September 1989 Hurricane Hugo hit Puerto Rico; only half the wild population of parrots survived.

100

53

47

53

40

23

16

1972

early 1989

late 1989
after Hurricane Hugo

1998

KIRIBATI

PITCAIRN

SOLOMON ISLANDS

VANUATU

FIJI

FRENCH POLYNESIA

NEW CALEDONIA

COOK ISLAND

NORFOLK ISLAND

Hong Kong

PHILIPPINES

SINGAPORE

INDONESIA

EAST TIMOR

PAPUA NEW GUINEA

The **Mauritius parakeet** is one of the most endangered parrots in the world, particularly as attempts at captive breeding have proved largely unsuccessful.

ZAMBIA

ZIMBABWE

NAMIBIA BOTSWANA

REUNION

MAURITIUS

AUSTRALIA

NEW ZEALAND

THREATENED PARROTS AND COCKATOOS

Number of species of parrot and cockatoo classified as critically endangered, endangered or vulnerable *2000*

A critically endangered species of:

parrot/parakeet/conure

lorikeet

macaw

cockatoo

16

11 – 15

6 – 10

3 – 5

1 – 2

none or no data

The flightless, nocturnal **kakapo parrot** has been reduced to a wild population of around 50 individuals. The parrots breed infrequently and are easy prey to introduced carnivorous species, such as rats. Conservation efforts have focused on relocating the remaining individuals to islands without predators and on supplementing their diet to encourage them to breed.

81

SEABIRDS

The term "seabird" is not a taxonomic classification, but simply a description of birds that live in a certain habitat, and exhibit certain physical characteristics and patterns of behavior. Many seabird species are, for example, good fliers, often exploiting prevailing winds to migrate extraordinary distances. Penguins and auks, though flightless, are strong and agile swimmers. Most seabirds catch fish and crustaceans near the ocean surface, but cormorants can dive up to 150 feet (46 metres) below the surface in search of prey. Some seabirds forage on land for insects, small rodents and rubbish. Skuas and frigatebirds harass smaller seabirds returning to land with fish, forcing their victim to drop its catch so that they can pluck it from the air before it hits the sea.

Seabirds usually nest in huge colonies, sometimes of over a million birds, on islands or cliffs where they are reasonably safe from native predatory mammals – although not always from "introduced" species. Seabirds have a low rate of reproduction, which makes them vulnerable to catastrophic events, such as oil pollution or sudden food shortages.

In the 19th century North Atlantic sailors caused the extinction of the great auk by killing whole colonies for their flesh and feathers. Seabirds are still exploited for their eggs in the Faroe Islands, Iceland, Greenland and Southeast Asia, and such "harvesting", if not properly controlled, can threaten their survival. Far out at sea, birds are still not safe from humans. Drift-nets, nicknamed "walls of death", used by large fishing boats, trap birds such as shearwaters, despite a 1992 UN moratorium on the use of nets more than 1.4 miles (2.5 km) long.

Long-line fishing also takes a huge toll of seabirds. Lines can be up to 62 miles (100 km) long, with more than 20,000 hooks. The bait on the hooks presents a ready meal for seabirds – and also the risk of becoming caught and drowned. Conservation organizations are working with the fishing industry to promote responsible fishing techniques, such as an effective bird-scarer over the fishing line, and the weighting of the line to ensure that it sinks rapidly.

Pollution is an insidious threat to seabirds. Oil-spills have contaminated Adelie Penguins in the Antarctic, and when the *Exxon Valdez* spilled 11 million gallons of crude oil into Prince William Sound in Alaska, thousands of seabirds died. Global climate change threatens all seabirds, because plankton, which are fundamental to the marine food chain, become less abundant when seawater warms.

Tuna fisheries have reported catching one seabird for every 200–300 hooks set on their long-lines. Some boats set as many as 20,000 hooks on each line.

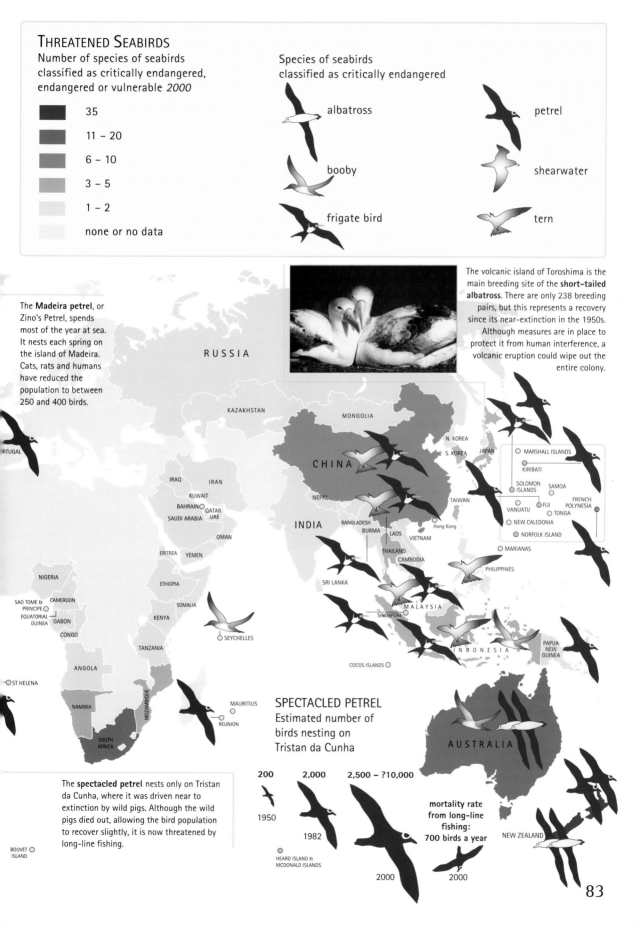

THREATENED SEABIRDS

Number of species of seabirds classified as critically endangered, endangered or vulnerable *2000*

- 35
- 11 – 20
- 6 – 10
- 3 – 5
- 1 – 2
- none or no data

Species of seabirds classified as critically endangered

- albatross
- booby
- frigate bird
- petrel
- shearwater
- tern

The volcanic island of Toroshima is the main breeding site of the **short-tailed albatross**. There are only 238 breeding pairs, but this represents a recovery since its near-extinction in the 1950s. Although measures are in place to protect it from human interference, a volcanic eruption could wipe out the entire colony.

The **Madeira petrel**, or Zino's Petrel, spends most of the year at sea. It nests each spring on the island of Madeira. Cats, rats and humans have reduced the population to between 250 and 400 birds.

SPECTACLED PETREL
Estimated number of birds nesting on Tristan da Cunha

200 — 1950

2,000 — 1982

2,500 – ?10,000 — 2000

mortality rate from long-line fishing: 700 birds a year — 2000

The **spectacled petrel** nests only on Tristan da Cunha, where it was driven near to extinction by wild pigs. Although the wild pigs died out, allowing the bird population to recover slightly, it is now threatened by long-line fishing.

RUSSIA
KAZAKHSTAN
MONGOLIA
N. KOREA
S. KOREA
JAPAN
CHINA
IRAQ
IRAN
KUWAIT
BAHRAIN
QATAR
UAE
SAUDI ARABIA
OMAN
NEPAL
TAIWAN
INDIA
BANGLADESH
BURMA
LAOS
VIETNAM
Hong Kong
THAILAND
CAMBODIA
ERITREA
YEMEN
SRI LANKA
PHILIPPINES
ETHIOPIA
SOMALIA
NIGERIA
CAMEROON
SAO TOME & PRINCIPE
EQUATORIAL GUINEA
GABON
CONGO
KENYA
MALAYSIA
SINGAPORE
TANZANIA
INDONESIA
PAPUA NEW GUINEA
ANGOLA
ST HELENA
NAMIBIA
MOZAMBIQUE
SOUTH AFRICA
MAURITIUS
REUNION
SEYCHELLES
COCOS ISLANDS
AUSTRALIA
NEW ZEALAND
MARIANAS
MARSHALL ISLANDS
KIRIBATI
SOLOMON ISLANDS
SAMOA
VANUATU
FIJI
TONGA
FRENCH POLYNESIA
NEW CALEDONIA
NORFOLK ISLAND
RTUGAL
BOUVET ISLAND
HEARD ISLAND & MCDONALD ISLANDS

MIGRATORY BIRDS

Most migrating birds breed in the northern hemisphere in early summer, hatch their young and then head south to escape the winter. Their mobility makes them difficult to study and there is still much to be discovered about bird migration. Many projects are underway, involving ring tagging and satellite tracking. More traditional methods, relying on teams of amateur bird spotters, have been greatly helped by the ability to communicate information swiftly over the internet.

The main routes adopted by migrating birds have been identified and named, but not all birds stick to a single route. Some start on one flyway and then cross to another, and many birds take a circular tour – flying out on one route and back on another. Most migrating birds rely on stopover sites, at which they can rest, feed, and fortify themselves for the next stage of their journey. Wetlands are perhaps the most important of these habitats, but many, such as those near the Mediterranean coast, are threatened by commercial development, drainage for agriculture, or, as in the case of Tunisia's Ichkeul National Park, the loss of their inflow of fresh water.

Climate change is also likely to have a damaging effect on wetlands. Changes in rainfall patterns could lead to some wetland areas drying out. And rising sea-levels, caused by the warming and expansion of the oceans and the increasingly rapid melting of the polar ice-caps, will inundate coastal wetlands. In the Arctic, birds face the threat of lost breeding grounds because a rise in average temperature is melting the permafrost, and will eventually cause trees to colonise what was open tundra.

Many migrating birds never arrive at their destination. Millions are shot down, especially by farmers in the Middle East and Africa, or hunters in southern Europe, where they are killed for sport. And if they escape the bullets, they still have to negotiate built-up areas, and avoid flying into skyscrapers or becoming entangled in power cables.

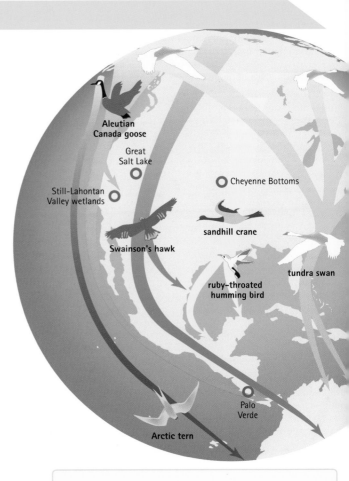

Aleutian
Canada goose

Great
Salt Lake

Cheyenne Bottoms

Still-Lahontan
Valley wetlands

sandhill crane

Swainson's hawk

tundra swan

ruby-throated
humming bird

Palo
Verde

Arctic tern

MIGRATION ROUTES
Main routes taken by
migrating birds to
escape northern winter

Routes in Americas:
- Pacific Flyway
- Central Flyway
- Mississippi Flyway
- Atlantic Flyway
- route of the Arctic tern

Routes in Europe and Africa:
- Iceland to northern Europe
- Siberia to northern Europe
- East Atlantic Flyway
- Mediterranean/Black Sea Flyway
- Asia–Africa Flyway
- route of the Arctic tern

Routes in Asia and Oceania:
- Central Asian–South Asian Flyway
- East Asian–Australian Flyway
- West Pacific Flyway

O   wetland site under threat
selected examples

    major threat from human hunters

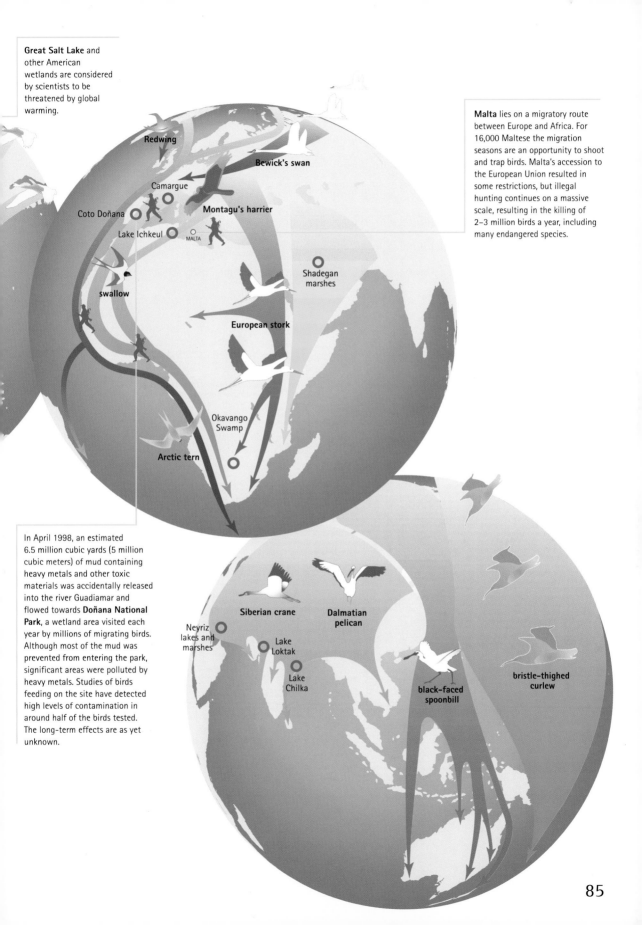

Great Salt Lake and other American wetlands are considered by scientists to be threatened by global warming.

Redwing

Bewick's swan

Camargue

Coto Doñana

Montagu's harrier

Lake Ichkeul

MALTA

Malta lies on a migratory route between Europe and Africa. For 16,000 Maltese the migration seasons are an opportunity to shoot and trap birds. Malta's accession to the European Union resulted in some restrictions, but illegal hunting continues on a massive scale, resulting in the killing of 2–3 million birds a year, including many endangered species.

Shadegan marshes

swallow

European stork

Okavango Swamp

Arctic tern

In April 1998, an estimated 6.5 million cubic yards (5 million cubic meters) of mud containing heavy metals and other toxic materials was accidentally released into the river Guadiamar and flowed towards **Doñana National Park**, a wetland area visited each year by millions of migrating birds. Although most of the mud was prevented from entering the park, significant areas were polluted by heavy metals. Studies of birds feeding on the site have detected high levels of contamination in around half of the birds tested. The long-term effects are as yet unknown.

Siberian crane

Dalmatian pelican

Neyriz lakes and marshes

Lake Loktak

Lake Chilka

black-faced spoonbill

bristle-thighed curlew

85

Issues of Conservation

"To achieve conservation results that are ecologically viable, it is necessary to conserve networks of key sites, migration corridors, and the ecological processes that maintain healthy ecosystems."

— WWF website, Endangered Spaces

ANIMAL BIODIVERSITY

There are probably about 10 million species in the kingdom of animals. About 1.2 million of them have been named and described by the scientific community, but the total number can only be estimated because much of the world has not yet been properly surveyed. New techniques are constantly being developed for examining previously uncharted regions that were thought to be barren. For example, remote-control submarines are revealing some of the remarkable species to be found in the ocean depths, and the diverse communities of bacteria, protists and fish to be found in hydro-thermal vents on the sea floor (see pages 30–31).

In lakes and oceans diversity is highest near the surface, particularly in the "photic" zone (the top 100 feet or 30 metres), where photosynthesis takes place. On land, diversity tends to be at its lowest in temperate and polar regions, possibly as a result of extinctions caused by the advance of glaciers during the recent ice-ages. In the tropics, where there is reliable moisture and warm, stable temperatures, animal diversity is much higher. Species living in these regions do not need the broad characteristics necessary for coping with varying conditions (such as drought, or winter temperatures) and adapt and diversify to suit local conditions (such as a particular type of tree, or ground cover). This leads both to a rich diversity and to a large number of endemic species. The endemic species shown on the map belong to groups that have been fairly well researched, but there are an even greater, and as yet uncounted, number of insects endemic to very small patches of land.

While the rate of extinction through natural processes is estimated as less than one species a year for every million species, habitat destruction has led to a current annual extinction rate of between 1,000 and 10,000 per million species. The disappearance of some species represents lost opportunities for exploiting genetic peculiarities that could have been harnessed for medicine and agriculture. A few will be "keystone" species, whose destruction will spell doom for entire communities.

Primates, such as the **chimpanzee**, along with other large mammals, tend to reproduce more slowly than smaller mammals, birds and reptiles. This makes them more vulnerable to natural disasters and human interference.

Isolated islands may not have a large number of species, but many will be endemic. Each of the Galapagos Islands is home to its own variation of species such as the **giant tortoise**, and the finch.

ANIMAL BIODIVERSITY
Number of mammals
per 10,000 square kilometers *2000*

- more than 100
- 51 – 100
- 21 – 50
- 1 – 20
- none or no data

- 100 or more endemic species of mammal
- 100 or more endemic species of bird
- 100 or more endemic species of reptile

TOTAL KNOWN SPECIES
Excluding fish and invertebrates *1999*

- 9,672 — birds
- 6,900 — reptiles
- 4,629 — mammals
- 4,522 — amphibians

Lemurs are endemic to the island of Madagascar. They have developed an amazing variety to fill a range of ecological niches. **Red-ruffed lemurs** live only in the deciduous forest of the Masoala Peninsula in northeastern Madagascar, where logging and trapping have reduced their numbers to between 1,000 and 10,000.

89

PLANT BIODIVERSITY

About 300,000 species of plants have been identified, out of an estimated total of 320,000. Recently developed genetic techniques have enabled botanists to distinguish much more precisely the differences between species of plants. Flowering plants are by far the most numerous – the result of successful co-evolution with the animals that pollinate them and disperse their seeds.

Biodiversity is assessed in terms both of the number of species in a given area, and their abundance. A forest with one dominant species of tree and a handful of individuals of other tree species is considered to have a lower biodiveristy than a forest with the same number of tree species occurring in roughly equal numbers. As with animals, the diversity of plants tends to be highest near the equator, where the sun is strongest. In general, though, the lower and more widely fluctuating temperatures at high altitude, mean that diversity tends to be lower on mountains than at sea level.

Natural habitats provide numerous benefits, including the prevention of soil erosion, filtering of pollutants from water and the exchange of gases with the atmosphere. Such "ecosystem services" are not always taken into account, however, when development plans are drawn up. Over-extraction of natural resources and the cultivation of a small number of fast-growing varieties of crops condemn ever-larger areas of the Earth's surface to low biodiversity.

Plants have evolved to grow even in water of varying salinity. **Pa–Hay–Okee** ("grassy waters"), an area of 2,200 sq miles (5,700 sq km) of unique wetland habitat, was declared the Everglades National Park in 1947.

NUMBER OF PLANT SPECIES
2001

270,000 — flowering plants

12,000 — ferns

550 — conifers

145 — cycads

1,000 — club mosses

16,000 — mosses and liverworts

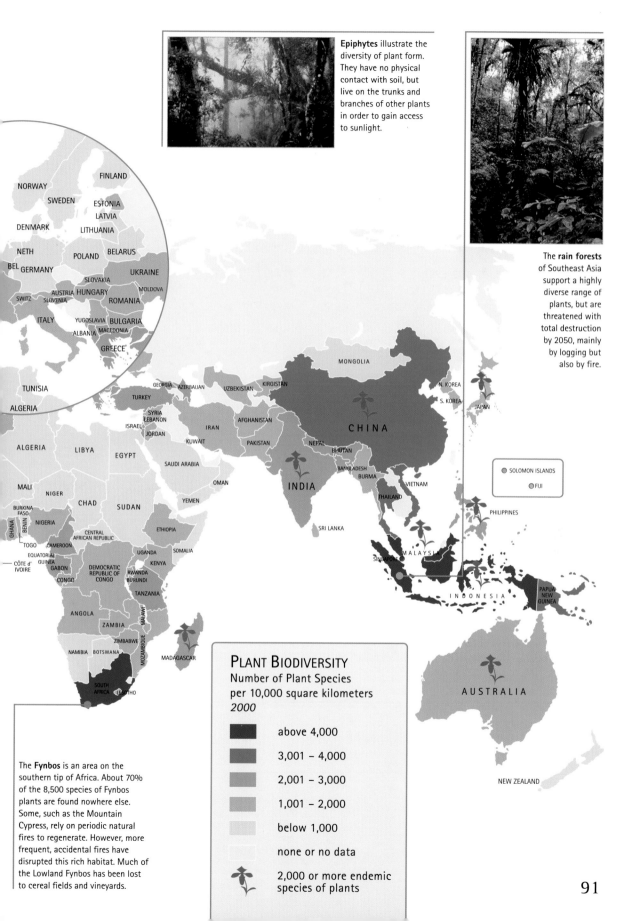

Epiphytes illustrate the diversity of plant form. They have no physical contact with soil, but live on the trunks and branches of other plants in order to gain access to sunlight.

The **rain forests** of Southeast Asia support a highly diverse range of plants, but are threatened with total destruction by 2050, mainly by logging but also by fire.

FINLAND
NORWAY
SWEDEN
ESTONIA
LATVIA
DENMARK
LITHUANIA
NETH
POLAND
BELARUS
BEL
GERMANY
UKRAINE
SLOVAKIA
AUSTRIA HUNGARY
MOLDOVA
SWITZ SLOVENIA
ITALY
ROMANIA
YUGOSLAVIA BULGARIA
ALBANIA MACEDONIA
GREECE

TUNISIA
ALGERIA

GEORGIA AZERBAIJAN
UZBEKISTAN
KIRGISTAN
MONGOLIA
N. KOREA
TURKEY
S. KOREA
JAPAN
SYRIA
LEBANON
ISRAEL
JORDAN
AFGHANISTAN
ALGERIA
LIBYA
EGYPT
IRAN
KUWAIT
SAUDI ARABIA
PAKISTAN
NEPAL
BHUTAN
CHINA
OMAN
INDIA
BANGLADESH
BURMA
VIETNAM
MALI
NIGER
YEMEN
THAILAND
BURKINA
FASO
CHAD
SUDAN
PHILIPPINES
GHANA BENIN
NIGERIA
SRI LANKA
SOLOMON ISLANDS
TOGO
CENTRAL
AFRICAN REPUBLIC
ETHIOPIA
FIJI
CAMEROON
EQUATORIAL GUINEA
CÔTE d'
IVOIRE
GABON
UGANDA
SOMALIA
SINGAPORE
MALAYSIA
DEMOCRATIC
REPUBLIC OF
CONGO
KENYA
CONGO
RWANDA
BURUNDI
TANZANIA
INDONESIA
PAPUA
NEW
GUINEA
ANGOLA
MALAWI
ZAMBIA
AUSTRALIA
ZIMBABWE
MOZAMBIQUE
NAMIBIA BOTSWANA
MADAGASCAR
SOUTH
AFRICA LESOTHO

NEW ZEALAND

PLANT BIODIVERSITY
Number of Plant Species per 10,000 square kilometers
2000

- above 4,000
- 3,001 – 4,000
- 2,001 – 3,000
- 1,001 – 2,000
- below 1,000
- none or no data
- 2,000 or more endemic species of plants

The **Fynbos** is an area on the southern tip of Africa. About 70% of the 8,500 species of Fynbos plants are found nowhere else. Some, such as the Mountain Cypress, rely on periodic natural fires to regenerate. However, more frequent, accidental fires have disrupted this rich habitat. Much of the Lowland Fynbos has been lost to cereal fields and vineyards.

91

With threatened and degraded habitats on every continent, conservation organizations face a daunting task. They have adopted different strategies in their attempts to cope with the seemingly impossible task of counteracting the bulldozer of development.

One approach has been to target key areas. Conservation International has identified 25 priority hotspots (see map) based on three criteria: species density, the number of endemic species in the area, and the level of threat they are experiencing. Around 44 percent of all vascular plant species and 70 percent of all non-fish vertebrates can be found in the 25 hotspots, which represent about 1.4 percent of the Earth's land surface.

The WWF has taken a slightly different approach to the problem of targeting its conservation efforts. It has identified 200 ecoregions, representing 25 distinctive habitats, ranging from lush tropical rainforest to temperate forest, dry savanna to arctic tundra, deserts to wetlands, and tropical to arctic marine environments. Further targeting has resulted in the Focal 25 (see map).

Wilderness areas – where 75 percent of the natural habit is undisturbed, and there is a density of no more than 13 people per square mile (5 people per sq km) – are also the focus of the attention of conservationists. Although the size of areas such as the Amazon and Congo rain forests makes them appear unassailable, the speed of development is giving cause for deep concern. If no action is taken to protect these regions, their ecology will become degraded through fragmentation and fire damage long before the forests have vanished completely.

Ecological conservation cannot be imposed by external organizations or even by national governments. It requires the cooperation of those living and working in the area, many of whom are dependent on the very activities the conservation groups are trying to stop. So, the emphasis now is on training, education and the promotion of sustainable industries.

The **Klamath–Siskiyou** temperate forest contains 30 conifer species and 131 endemic plants, including the ancient Brewer spruce, the Port Orford cedar, and the insect-eating cobra lily.

Bering Sea

Klamath–Siskiyou Forests

California Floristic Province

Chihuahuan Desert

Gulf of California

Rivers and Streams of the American Southwest

Everglades and Florida Keys

Mesoamerica Caribbean Reef

Mesoamerica

Caribbean

Galapagos Islands

Flooded Forests of the Amazon

Brazil's Cerrado

Tropical Forests of the Northern Andes

Chocó/Darien/ Western Equator

Central Chile

Atlantic Forest

Brazil's Atlantic Forest

Polynesia/Micronesia

Southwestern Amazon Rainforests

Valdivian Temperate Forest

The Atlantic forest has been reduced to around 7 percent of its original terrain, with some so fragmented as to make its survival unlikely. The **golden lion tamarin**, found nowhere else, is just one of nine critically endangered mammals in this hotspot.

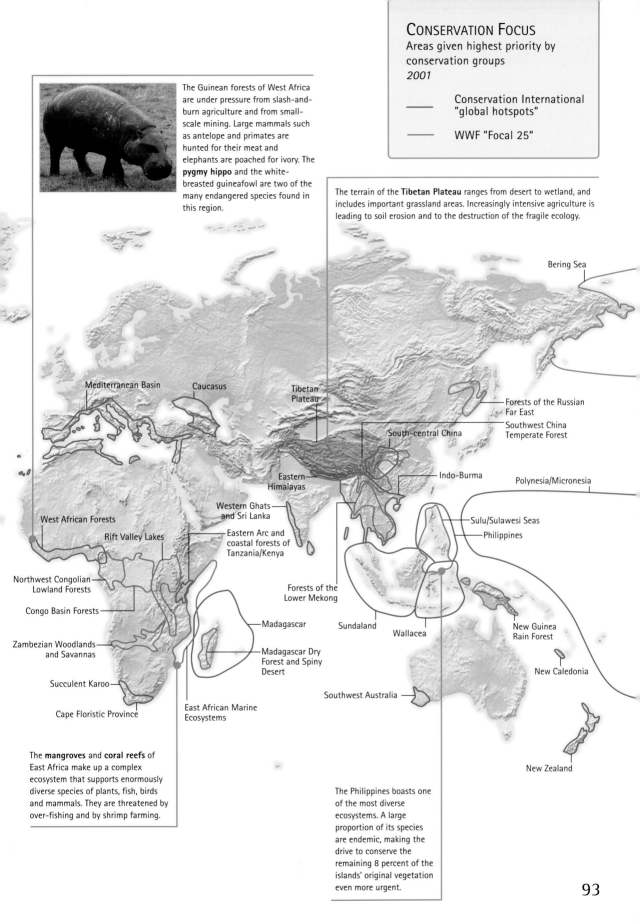

The Guinean forests of West Africa are under pressure from slash-and-burn agriculture and from small-scale mining. Large mammals such as antelope and primates are hunted for their meat and elephants are poached for ivory. The **pygmy hippo** and the white-breasted guineafowl are two of the many endangered species found in this region.

The terrain of the **Tibetan Plateau** ranges from desert to wetland, and includes important grassland areas. Increasingly intensive agriculture is leading to soil erosion and to the destruction of the fragile ecology.

Bering Sea

Mediterranean Basin

Caucasus

Tibetan Plateau

Forests of the Russian Far East

Southwest China Temperate Forest

South-central China

Indo-Burma

Polynesia/Micronesia

Eastern Himalayas

Western Ghats and Sri Lanka

West African Forests

Rift Valley Lakes

Eastern Arc and coastal forests of Tanzania/Kenya

Sulu/Sulawesi Seas

Philippines

Northwest Congolian Lowland Forests

Forests of the Lower Mekong

Congo Basin Forests

Madagascar

Sundaland

Wallacea

New Guinea Rain Forest

Zambezian Woodlands and Savannas

Madagascar Dry Forest and Spiny Desert

New Caledonia

Succulent Karoo

Southwest Australia

Cape Floristic Province

East African Marine Ecosystems

New Zealand

The **mangroves** and **coral reefs** of East Africa make up a complex ecosystem that supports enormously diverse species of plants, fish, birds and mammals. They are threatened by over-fishing and by shrimp farming.

The Philippines boasts one of the most diverse ecosystems. A large proportion of its species are endemic, making the drive to conserve the remaining 8 percent of the islands' original vegetation even more urgent.

CONSERVING ANIMALS

How best to save threatened animal species has been a fiercely contested subject. In an ideal world all animals would be conserved in their natural habitat, but despite the efforts of conservationists the predicted rate of habitat destruction could result in as many as 2,000 species needing support through captive breeding if they are to survive. The conservation movement is now focusing on captive breeding undertaken alongside programs to conserve and manage the habitats in which the species thrive.

In order to keep a species genetically diverse and healthy, populations of between 250 and 500 are necessary, with breeding between animals in different centres. The breeding of endangered animals is in many cases managed by dedicated international programs, which keep detailed studbooks.

There are currently around 250,000 animals in the world's zoos, but many of the species most prolifically represented are not the most threatened. Zoos are expensive to run, and although some zoos receive funding from national or local governments, most rely largely on ticket sales for their income. About 600 million people visit a zoo each year, but many zoos are faced with a dilemma – whether to provide a wide range of the more popular animals in order to attract more visitors, or to concentrate on threatened species.

Sometimes, animals bred in captivity can be released into the wild. This has been done successfully with the Arabian oryx (see pages 54–55) and several other species, but much depends on how well these released animals can be protected in the wild, and whether there is any suitable habitat left into which to release them.

The **Durrell Wildlife Conservation Trust**, based at Jersey Zoo, runs captive-breeding programs and conservation projects around the world in support of critically endangered animals. These include the **Alaotran gentle lemur**, whose habitat is reduced to a single area of wetland in Madagascar, which was declared a Ramsar Site in 2003.

The **Mallorcan midwife toad** was thought extinct until 1980. It has since been bred in captivity by Durrell Wildlife Conservation Trust and others, and reintroduced into the island's northern mountains. The male incubates strings of eggs wound around his legs.

The habitat of the **black lion tamarin** is Brazil's Atlantic Forest, less than a tenth of which is left. Several of the species have been successfully bred at Jersey Zoo, but have not adapted as well as hoped on release into the Brazilian forest. Conservationists are now focusing on the strategy of replanting forest to create link corridors between isolated groups of tamarins.

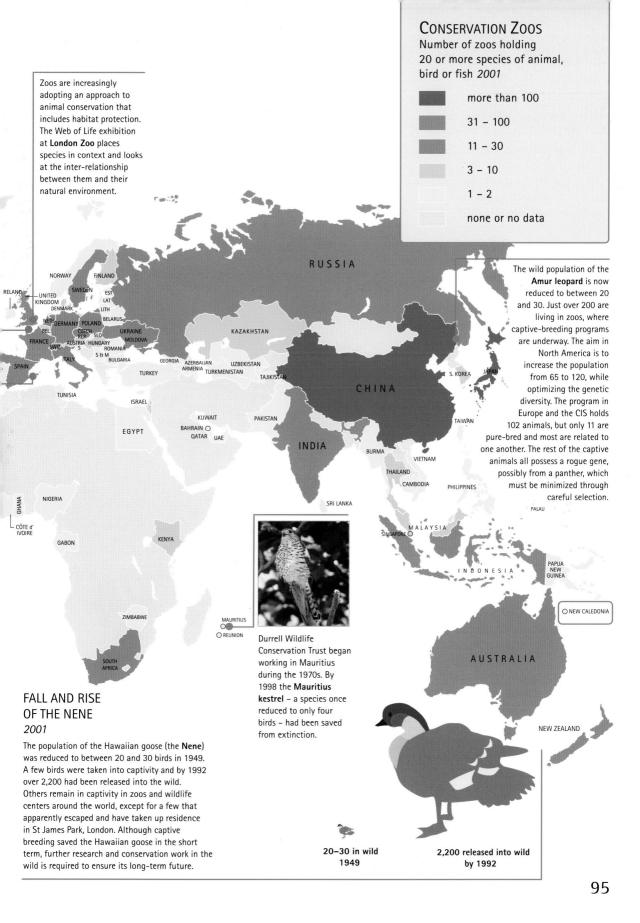

Zoos are increasingly adopting an approach to animal conservation that includes habitat protection. The Web of Life exhibition at **London Zoo** places species in context and looks at the inter-relationship between them and their natural environment.

CONSERVATION ZOOS
Number of zoos holding 20 or more species of animal, bird or fish *2001*

▮	more than 100
▮	31 – 100
▮	11 – 30
▮	3 – 10
▮	1 – 2
▮	none or no data

The wild population of the **Amur leopard** is now reduced to between 20 and 30. Just over 200 are living in zoos, where captive-breeding programs are underway. The aim in North America is to increase the population from 65 to 120, while optimizing the genetic diversity. The program in Europe and the CIS holds 102 animals, but only 11 are pure-bred and most are related to one another. The rest of the captive animals all possess a rogue gene, possibly from a panther, which must be minimized through careful selection.

Durrell Wildlife Conservation Trust began working in Mauritius during the 1970s. By 1998 the **Mauritius kestrel** – a species once reduced to only four birds – had been saved from extinction.

FALL AND RISE OF THE NENE
2001

The population of the Hawaiian goose (the **Nene**) was reduced to between 20 and 30 birds in 1949. A few birds were taken into captivity and by 1992 over 2,200 had been released into the wild. Others remain in captivity in zoos and wildlife centers around the world, except for a few that apparently escaped and have taken up residence in St James Park, London. Although captive breeding saved the Hawaiian goose in the short term, further research and conservation work in the wild is required to ensure its long-term future.

20–30 in wild 1949

2,200 released into wild by 1992

CONSERVING PLANTS

Botanic gardens are the zoos of the plant world. There are about 1,600 of them, containing roughly a quarter of all species of flowering plants and ferns. They are visited each year by about 150 million people worldwide and, as with zoos, public education is an important function. Some gardens incorporate herbaria, where plant specimens are dried and held to provide a permanent reference for plant diversity. Botanic gardens often also maintain seed banks. Seeds are only viable for a certain period, so drying and low-temperature storage ("cryopreservation") is used to prevent them germinating or rotting .

Governments around the world have declared nature reserves in order to protect important habitats. However, the size of a protected area is significant. Small reserves hold fewer individuals of any one plant species, which leads to a greater risk of that plant becoming extinct. Reserves need to be close to each other, or connected by similar habitat, to allow pollination and seed dispersal between them.

Preventing frequent fires is important for most plants. In the tundra the risk of fire is relatively low, plant diversity is modest and there is limited scope for agriculture. In consequence, fewer protected areas have been designated there.

Invasive plants can overwhelm ecologically balanced native flora. Physical destruction of invasive plants, pesticides and the introduction of herbivores and parasites are all used to control invasive species. Genetic pollution is a more recent hazard. Genetically modified crops could, in theory, pollinate natural relatives, with the result that genes from organisms as exotic as fish are spread to wild plants.

Eco-labelling of timber can exploit market mechanisms to promote conservation. The Forest Stewardship Council administers a certification scheme for timber extracted according to strict ecological principles. These aim either to leave forests largely intact or to give the species that are cut down an opportunity to regenerate. The success of such conservation strategies relies on harnessing the knowledge of local people about the plants around them.

Over 900 invasive species of plant, such as the **Japanese knotweed**, threaten the native flora of the USA.

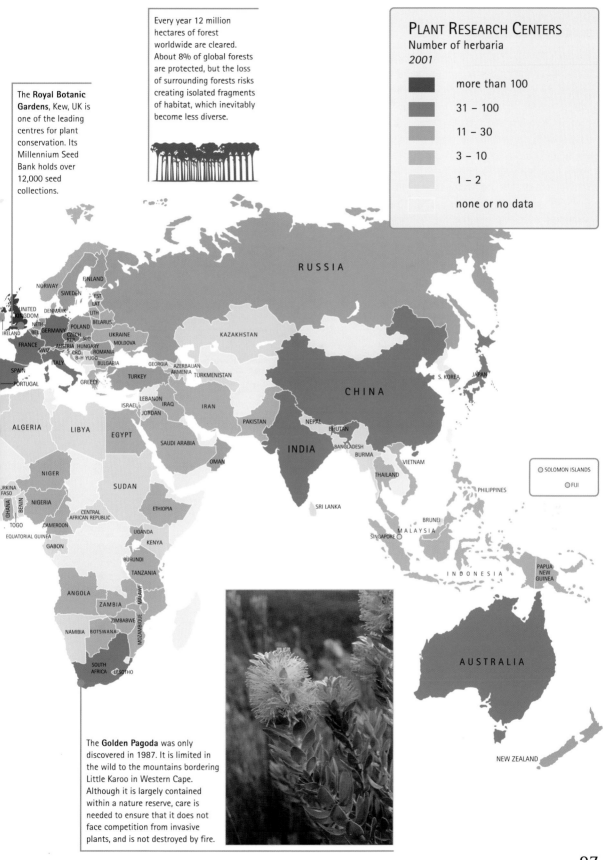

The **Royal Botanic Gardens**, Kew, UK is one of the leading centres for plant conservation. Its Millennium Seed Bank holds over 12,000 seed collections.

Every year 12 million hectares of forest worldwide are cleared. About 8% of global forests are protected, but the loss of surrounding forests risks creating isolated fragments of habitat, which inevitably become less diverse.

PLANT RESEARCH CENTERS
Number of herbaria
2001

- more than 100
- 31 – 100
- 11 – 30
- 3 – 10
- 1 – 2
- none or no data

RUSSIA

NORWAY
FINLAND
SWEDEN
EST
LAT
LITH
DENMARK
UNITED KINGDOM
IRELAND
NETH-
BEL GERMANY POLAND
BELARUS
FRANCE CZECH SLO
REP
SWITZ AUSTRIA HUNGARY UKRAINE
S CRO- MOLDOVA
B-H YUGO ROMANIA
ITALY BULGARIA
SPAIN
PORTUGAL
GREECE
GEORGIA AZERBAIJAN
ARMENIA
TURKEY TURKMENISTAN

KAZAKHSTAN

S. KOREA JAPAN

LEBANON
ISRAEL IRAQ
JORDAN
IRAN
PAKISTAN

CHINA

NEPAL
BHUTAN
BANGLADESH
INDIA BURMA
VIETNAM

ALGERIA LIBYA EGYPT
SAUDI ARABIA
OMAN

THAILAND

PHILIPPINES

NIGER
URKINA
FASO
GHANA BENIN NIGERIA
TOGO CAMEROON
EQUATORIAL GUINEA
GABON

SUDAN
CENTRAL AFRICAN REPUBLIC
ETHIOPIA
UGANDA
KENYA
BURUNDI

SRI LANKA

BRUNEI
MALAYSIA
SINGAPORE

○ SOLOMON ISLANDS
○ FIJI

TANZANIA
ANGOLA
MALAWI
ZAMBIA
NAMIBIA BOTSWANA ZIMBABWE
MOZAMBIQUE
SOUTH AFRICA LESOTHO

INDONESIA

PAPUA NEW GUINEA

AUSTRALIA

NEW ZEALAND

The **Golden Pagoda** was only discovered in 1987. It is limited in the wild to the mountains bordering Little Karoo in Western Cape. Although it is largely contained within a nature reserve, care is needed to ensure that it does not face competition from invasive plants, and is not destroyed by fire.

CONSERVING DOMESTIC BREEDS

Humans have domesticated around 40 animal species. Over 12,000 years, thousands of different breeds have developed through selective breeding of these species as well as environmental factors. In recent decades, high-yielding breeds have been favored, with the result that other breeds are endangered or extinct. Nearly a third of domestic animal breeds are threatened by extinction. On average, two breeds are disappearing every week.

Domestic animal diversity is an important component of global biodiversity. Of the 6,500 or so breeds identified by the UN Food and Agriculture Organization (FAO), around 400 are "intensively developed": they produce high yields, but they also require a high level of maintenance, such as purpose-built shelters and specialized feed stuffs. The majority of the world's people, however, still rely on breeds that require minimum shelter and natural grazing, but do not necessarily give a high yield of milk or meat. While there is a global need to increase food production, the promotion of high-yield breeds that cannot cope with adverse local conditions is not the answer.

The preservation of a wide variety of breeds provides a genetic pool from which scientists can develop animals to meet future needs. Climate change, with its attendant impact on local environmental conditions may require the development of drought-resistant breeds. The specific genes that provide certain breeds with resistance to disease can be identified and introduced into higher-yielding breeds. As food fashions change, for health and cultural reasons, breeds can be developed to meet demand.

The FAO World Watch List assesses the viability of specific breeds within a country. Some populations have been deemed too low for survival. Others are in the "critical" or "endangered" category. This draws the attention of national organizations to threatened breeds within their borders, but it also produces anomalies. Countries in Africa, where data is not available on many breeds, register relatively few threatened breeds. On the other hand, European countries register a large number of threatened breeds because efforts are being made to conserve them.

The **angler sattelschwein** is now reduced to only 35 breeding females.

BREEDS EXTINCT OR UNDER THREAT
selected species *1999*

- extinct
- critical or critical-maintained
- endangered or endangered-maintained
- not at risk
- unknown

cattle
1479 breeds

295 255
106
193
630

THREATENED DOMESTIC BREEDS

Number of species of domestic animal classified as critical, endangered, critical maintained or endangered maintained *2000*

	100 or more
	50 – 99
	20 – 49
	10 – 19
	1 – 9
	none
	no data

Critical: 100 or fewer breeding females, 5 or fewer breeding males, or a population of under 121 and decreasing, with the percentage of breeding females below 80 percent.
Endangered: 101–1000 breeding females, 6–20 breeding males, or a population of 81–99 and increasing, with the percentage of breeding females above 80 percent.
Critical maintained/Endangered maintained: critical or endangered populations for which active conservation programs are in place or populations are maintained by commercial companies or research institutions.

Number of extinct breeds:

- 20 or more (number given)
- 10 – 19
- 5 – 9

The **red Maasai sheep** is genetically resistant to intestinal worms. Scientists working to identify and isolate the gene hope to transfer immunity to other breeds.

goats
587 breeds
17
31
166 · 70
303

sheep
1495 breeds
181
391 · 68
199
656

pigs
649 breeds
111 · 151
223 · 58
106

chickens
734 breeds
32
141 · 101
195 · 265

Industrialized countries imported over 25,700 live primates in 1997, largely for use in research laboratories. Trade in other animals, in particular parrots and reptiles, is mostly driven by the pet trade, with 235,336 parrots legally imported in 1997, a third of them into Spain. There is also a large trade in reptile skins, now fashionable for clothes and accessories. Over 200,000 alligator skins are sold each year, although many of these are from farmed, rather than wild, animals. Reptile farming practices in some countries are brutal, and include skinning snakes alive, supposedly to obtain more supple skins.

The Convention on International Trade in Endangered Species of Wild Fauna and Flora (CITES) came into force in January 1975 and currently has over 150 signatory states. Under the convention, these states agree to ban commercial international trade in some species of animal and plant and to monitor trade in others. Export and import licenses have to be issued for species covered by the convention, and trade statistics reported annually to the CITES Trade Database, managed by the World Conservation Monitoring Centre in Cambridge, UK. Compliance with the reporting requirements is by no means universal, however, with many countries failing to send in even 50 percent of the required reports.

This map (and that on pages 102–103) therefore reflects legal trade, sanctioned under CITES. It does not include the billions of dollars worth of illegal trading conducted worldwide. Nor does it indicate the mortality rate among those animals licensed for live export and import. What it does show, however, is the extent of the legal trade in species considered at risk. It also identifies the major importing countries, whose demand is driving the trade.

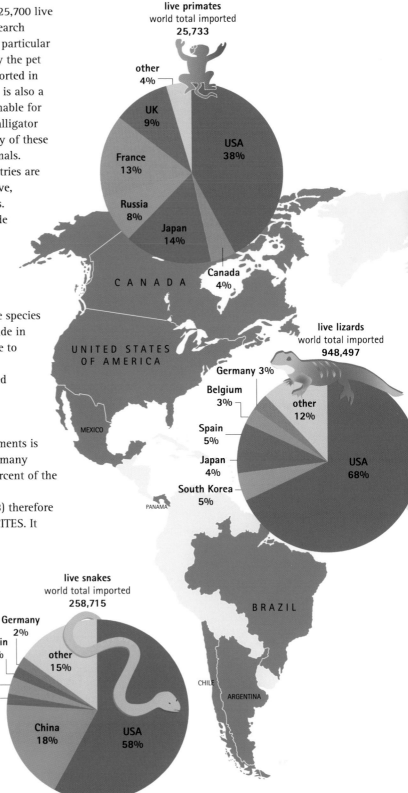

live primates
world total imported
25,733

other 4%
UK 9%
France 13%
Russia 8%
Japan 14%
USA 38%
Canada 4%

live lizards
world total imported
948,497

Germany 3%
Belgium 3%
Spain 5%
Japan 4%
South Korea 5%
other 12%
USA 68%

live snakes
world total imported
258,715

Germany 2%
Spain 2%
France 3%
Japan 2%
other 15%
China 18%
USA 58%

CANADA
UNITED STATES OF AMERICA
MEXICO
PANAMA
BRAZIL
CHILE
ARGENTINA

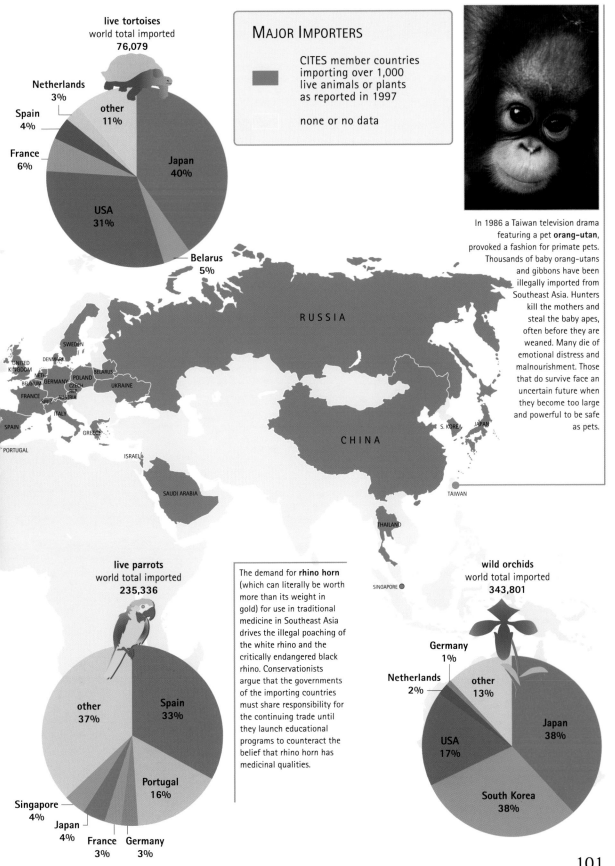

live tortoises
world total imported
76,079

- Netherlands 3%
- Spain 4%
- France 6%
- other 11%
- Japan 40%
- USA 31%
- Belarus 5%

MAJOR IMPORTERS

CITES member countries importing over 1,000 live animals or plants as reported in 1997

none or no data

In 1986 a Taiwan television drama featuring a pet **orang-utan**, provoked a fashion for primate pets. Thousands of baby orang-utans and gibbons have been illegally imported from Southeast Asia. Hunters kill the mothers and steal the baby apes, often before they are weaned. Many die of emotional distress and malnourishment. Those that do survive face an uncertain future when they become too large and powerful to be safe as pets.

SWEDEN
DENMARK
UNITED KINGDOM
BELARUS
NETH.
GERMANY POLAND
BELGIUM
CZECH REP. UKRAINE
FRANCE SWITZ. AUSTRIA
ITALY
SPAIN
GREECE
PORTUGAL
ISRAEL
SAUDI ARABIA

RUSSIA

CHINA

S. KOREA JAPAN

TAIWAN

THAILAND

SINGAPORE

live parrots
world total imported
235,336

- other 37%
- Spain 33%
- Portugal 16%
- Singapore 4%
- Japan 4%
- France 3%
- Germany 3%

The demand for **rhino horn** (which can literally be worth more than its weight in gold) for use in traditional medicine in Southeast Asia drives the illegal poaching of the white rhino and the critically endangered black rhino. Conservationists argue that the governments of the importing countries must share responsibility for the continuing trade until they launch educational programs to counteract the belief that rhino horn has medicinal qualities.

wild orchids
world total imported
343,801

- Germany 1%
- Netherlands 2%
- other 13%
- Japan 38%
- USA 17%
- South Korea 38%

EXPORT TRADE

The financial rewards from the export of valuable wild animals and plants are considerable. Around 30,000 species are included in the Convention on International Trade in Endangered Species of Wild Fauna and Flora (CITES). For species threatened with extinction, trade is banned except in exceptional circumstances. The convention also includes species for which trade needs to be controlled in order to prevent risk of extinction. Finally, it includes species protected in at least one country, where that country has asked other CITES parties for assistance in controlling trade worldwide.

Although the Convention regularly revises the list of species it covers, it is largely the responsibility of each member state to establish the appropriate maximum number of export licenses that can be issued for a species within its territory.

Even where appropriate licensing quotas have been established, they are difficult to enforce. CITES urges countries to designate a small number of ports of exit and entry, and to train specialized enforcement officers to help identify the species being traded. Little has been done in this regard, however, although measures taken in the USA, where only nine ports are authorized to handle wildlife exports and imports, do seem to have reduced illegal trade.

The organization TRAFFIC, the trade monitoring program of WWF and IUCN-The World Conservation Union, was set up in the 1970s to assist in the implementation of CITES. In recent years it has expanded its role to look not only at trade covered by the convention but at how international sectors, including the fisheries and timber trades, impact on whole regions.

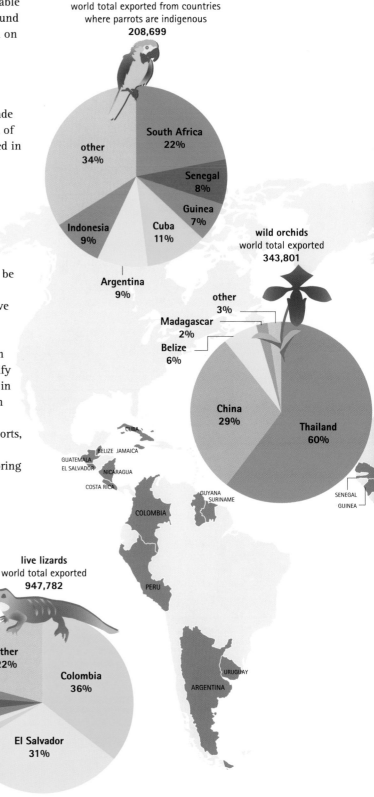

live parrots
world total exported from countries where parrots are indigenous
208,699

- South Africa 22%
- other 34%
- Senegal 8%
- Guinea 7%
- Cuba 11%
- Indonesia 9%
- Argentina 9%

wild orchids
world total exported
343,801

- other 3%
- Madagascar 2%
- Belize 6%
- China 29%
- Thailand 60%

live lizards
world total exported
947,782

- Ghana 2%
- other 22%
- Colombia 36%
- Tanzania 3%
- Togo 3%
- Suriname 2%
- El Salvador 31%
- Nicaragua 2%

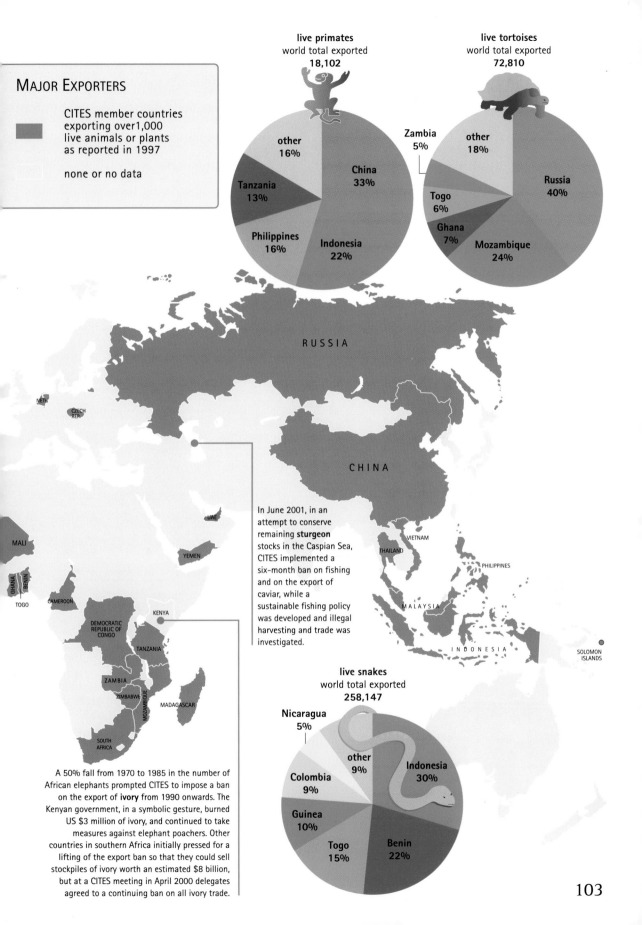

live primates
world total exported
18,102

- China 33%
- Indonesia 22%
- Philippines 16%
- Tanzania 13%
- other 16%

live tortoises
world total exported
72,810

- Russia 40%
- Mozambique 24%
- other 18%
- Ghana 7%
- Togo 6%
- Zambia 5%

MAJOR EXPORTERS

CITES member countries exporting over 1,000 live animals or plants as reported in 1997

none or no data

RUSSIA

NETH.

CZECH REP.

CHINA

UAE

MALI

YEMEN

VIETNAM

THAILAND

PHILIPPINES

GHANA

BENIN

TOGO

CAMEROON

KENYA

DEMOCRATIC REPUBLIC OF CONGO

TANZANIA

ZAMBIA

ZIMBABWE

MOZAMBIQUE

MADAGASCAR

SOUTH AFRICA

MALAYSIA

INDONESIA

SOLOMON ISLANDS

In June 2001, in an attempt to conserve remaining **sturgeon** stocks in the Caspian Sea, CITES implemented a six-month ban on fishing and on the export of caviar, while a sustainable fishing policy was developed and illegal harvesting and trade was investigated.

A 50% fall from 1970 to 1985 in the number of African elephants prompted CITES to impose a ban on the export of **ivory** from 1990 onwards. The Kenyan government, in a symbolic gesture, burned US $3 million of ivory, and continued to take measures against elephant poachers. Other countries in southern Africa initially pressed for a lifting of the export ban so that they could sell stockpiles of ivory worth an estimated $8 billion, but at a CITES meeting in April 2000 delegates agreed to a continuing ban on all ivory trade.

live snakes
world total exported
258,147

- Indonesia 30%
- Benin 22%
- Togo 15%
- Guinea 10%
- Colombia 9%
- other 9%
- Nicaragua 5%

103

WORLD TABLES

7

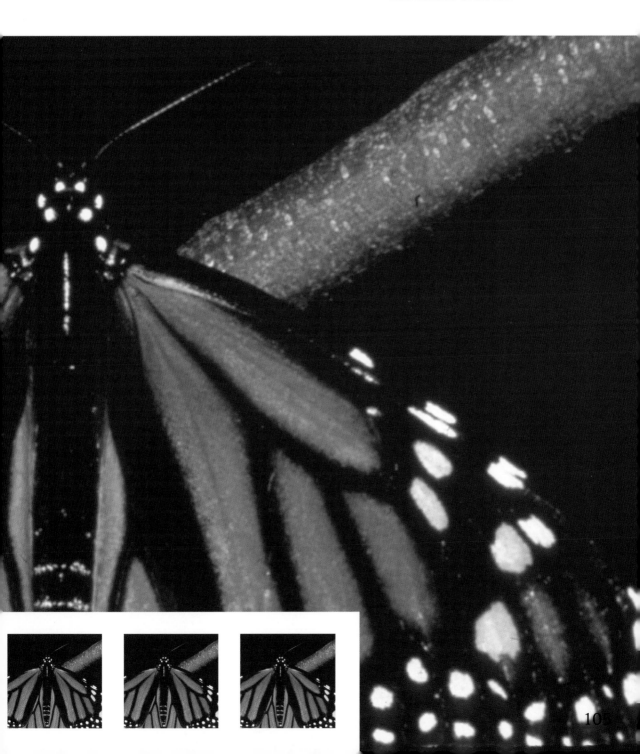

PROTECTED ECOSYSTEMS AND BIODIVERSITY

Country	1 LAND AREA 000 hectares	2 TROPICAL FOREST 000 hectares	% protected	3 TEMPERATE FOREST 000 hectares	% protected	4 MANGROVES 000 hectares	% protected	5 WETLANDS 000 hectares protected
Afghanistan	65,209	0	0	2,076	0	0	0	–
Albania	2,740	0	0	1,066	1.2	0	0	20
Algeria	238,174	0	0	2,694	3.7	0	0	1,866
Angola	124,670	37,564	2.6	0	0	125*	0	–
Argentina	273,669	4,360	5.5	19,094	10.1	0	0	2,670
Armenia	2,820	0	0	355	10.1	0	0	492
Australia	768,230	14,088	7.3	22,877	14.1	4,902	5.2	5,310
Austria	8,273	0	0	3,593	20.9	0	0	118
Azerbaijan	8,660	0	0	1,133	0	0	0	100
Bahamas	1,390	–	–	–	–	–	–	33
Bahrain	68	–	–	–	–	–	–	7
Bangladesh	13,017	862	3.7	0	0	440	8.3	606
Barbados	43	–	–	–	–	–	–	–
Belarus	20,748	0	0	6,280	6.5	0	0	204
Belgium	3,023	0	0	687	7.8	0	0	8
Belize	2,280	1,440	43.6	0	0	30	9.6	7
Benin	11,062	1,516	18.2	0	0	2*	0	139
Bhutan	4,700	966	22.9	1,129	37.6	0	0	–
Bolivia	108,438	68,638	12.1	0	0	0	0	6,518
Bosnia-Herzegovina	5,100	0	0	2,303	1	0	0	7
Botswana	56,673	12,123	19.9	0	0	0	0	6,864
Brazil	845,651	301,273	6.9	2,613	6.9	1,340	28.4	6,346
Brunei	580	–	–	–	–	–	–	–
Bulgaria	11,055	0	0	3,787	5.9	0	0	3
Burkina Faso	27,360	0	0	0	0	0	0	299
Burma	65,755	20,661	0.8	9,574	2	379*	0	–
Burundi	2,568	219	18.2	0	0	0	0	1
Cambodia	17,652	11,516	25.6	0	0	47	66.5	55
Cameroon	46,540	20,009	6	0	0	227	1.9	–
Canada	922,097	0	0	404,313	7.9	0	0	13,052
Cape Verde	–	–	–	–	–	–	–	–
Central African Rep.	62,298	17,101	20.1	0	0	0	0	–
Chad	125,920	3,516	3.6	0	0	0	0	1,843
Chile	74,880	0	0	14,526	27.1	0	0	100
China	932,641	109	13	82,710	3.9	36*	0	2,548
Colombia	103,870	53,186	10.8	0	0	368	22.2	439
Comoros	220	–	–	–	–	–	–	0
Congo	34,150	24,321	4.4	0	0	19	75.8	439
Congo, Dem. Rep.	226,705	135,071	6.6	0	0	22	0	866
Costa Rica	5,106	1,464	44.8	0	0	53	1.9	313
Côte-d'Ivoire	31,800	2,702	22.8	0	0	64*	0	19
Croatia	5,592	0	0	1,391	9.9	0	0	80
Cuba	10,982	1,761	15.3	0	0	767	7	452

 Sources: Col 1: *World Resources 1998-1999*, Table 11.2; Col 2 & 3: *World Resources 2000-2001*, Table FG.2; Col 4: *World Resources 1998-1999*, Table 11.2 and * *World Resources 2000-2001*, Table CMI.3; Col 5: Wetlands International, August 2002

SPECIES DENSITY Number of species per million hectares					Countries
6 MAMMALS	7 BIRDS	8 REPTILES	9 AMPHIBIANS	10 PLANTS	
31	59	26	2	1,008	Afghanistan
48	162	22	9	2,139	Albania
15	32	13	2	520	Algeria
56	156	–	–	1,055	Angola
50	140	37	24	1,463	Argentina
59	169	36	5	–	Armenia
29	72	83	23	1,741	Australia
41	106	7	10	1,537	Austria
49	122	26	5	2,109	Azerbaijan
–	–	–	–	–	Bahamas
–	–	–	–	–	Bahrain
45	122	49	8	2,074	Bangladesh
–	–	–	–	–	Barbados
27	81	3	4	772	Belarus
40	125	6	12	1,073	Belgium
95	271	81	24	2,200	Belize
85	138	–	–	990	Benin
59	269	11	14	3,281	Bhutan
67	–	45	26	3,885	Bolivia
42	127	16	9	–	Bosnia-Herzegovina
43	101	41	10	563	Botswana
45	162	53	63	6,058	Brazil
–	–	–	–	–	Brunei
37	108	15	8	1,615	Bulgaria
49	112	–	–	369	Burkina Faso
62	216	51	19	1,742	Burma
76	322	–	–	1,783	Burundi
47	118	32	11	–	Cambodia
114	193	51	53	2,310	Cameroon
20	44	4	4	335	Canada
–	–	–	–	–	Cape Verde
53	137	33	12	921	Central African Rep.
27	75	1	–	322	Chad
22	71	20	12	1,269	Chile
41	114	35	30	3,340	China
75	356	124	143	10,735	Colombia
–	–	–	–	–	Comoros
62	140	–	–	1,870	Congo
74	153	62	13	1,818	Congo, Dem. Rep.
120	350	125	98	7,074	Costa Rica
73	170	–	–	1,163	Côte-d'Ivoire
43	126	16	11	–	Croatia
14	62	47	25	2,949	Cuba

PROTECTED ECOSYSTEMS AND BIODIVERSITY

Country	1 LAND AREA 000 hectares	2 TROPICAL FOREST 000 hectares	2 TROPICAL FOREST % protected	3 TEMPERATE FOREST 000 hectares	3 TEMPERATE FOREST % protected	4 MANGROVES 000 hectares	4 MANGROVES % protected	5 WETLANDS 000 hectares protected
Cyprus	930	–	–	–	–	–	–	2
Czech Republic	7,728	0	0	2,481	27.5	0	0	42
Denmark	4,243	0	0	459	4.2	0	0	2,283
Djibouti	2,320	–	–	–	–	–	–	–
Dominican Republic	4,838	1,171	16.9	0	0	70	52.1	20
Ecuador	27,684	13,508	23.9	0	0	238	14.2	83
Egypt	99,545	4	0	134	0	86*	0	106
El Salvador	2,072	111	4.5	0	0	45	0	2
Equatorial Guinea	2,805	1,749	0	0	0	25	0	–
Eritrea	10,100	1	0	0	0	58*	0	–
Estonia	4,227	0	0	1,524	6.7	0	0	216
Ethiopia	100,000	11,937	18.8	0	0	0	0	–
Fiji	1,827	641	1	0	0	52	0	–
Finland	30,459	0	0	25,309	5.8	0	0	139
France	55,010	0	0	10,831	13.7	0	0	795
Gabon	25,767	21,481	3.6	0	0	147	3	1,080
Gambia	1,000	188	5.1	0	0	51	4.8	20
Georgia	6,970	0	0	3,158	0	0	0	34
Germany	34,927	0	0	10,401	24.8	0	0	829
Ghana	22,754	1,694	7.1	0	0	0	0	178
Greece	12,890	0	0	4,423	1.7	0	0	164
Guatemala	10,843	3,862	31.9	0	0	16	16.7	503
Guinea	24,572	3,073	1.1	0	0	316	0	4,779
Guinea Bissau	2,812	1,141	0	0	0	317	0	39
Guyana	19,685	17,844	1.3	0	0	159	0	–
Haiti	2,756	64	2	0	0	0	0	–
Honduras	11,189	5,273	18.3	0	0	231	42.2	172
Hungary	9,234	0	0	777	26.1	0	0	154
Iceland	10,025	0	0	–	–	–	–	59
India	297,319	44,450	8.9	9,260	8.3	304	49.6	195
Indonesia	181,157	88,744	20.9	0	0	2,390	32.8	243
Iran	162,200	0	0	2,348	12	21*	0	1,476
Iraq	43,737	–	–	–	–	–	–	–
Ireland	6,889	0	0	457	2.1	0	0	67
Israel	2,062	–	–	–	–	–	–	0
Italy	29,406	0	0	6,757	6.1	0	0	57
Jamaica	1,083	399	20.5	0	0	9	10.8	6
Japan	37,652	0	0	5,677	9.7	0.4*	0	84
Jordan	8,893	–	–	–	–	–	–	7
Kazakhstan	267,073	0	0	2,638	9.6	0	0	–
Kenya	56,914	3,423	8.3	0	0	0	0	91
Kirgistan	19,180	0	0	785	0.2	0	0	–
Korea (North)	12,041	0	0	3,967	1.1	0	0	–

Sources: Col 1: *World Resources 1998-1999*, Table 11.2; Col 2 & 3: *World Resources 2000-2001*, Table FG.2; Col 4: *World Resources 1998-1999*, Table 11.2 and * *World Resources 2000-2001*, Table CMI.3; Col 5: Wetlands International, August 2002

SPECIES DENSITY — Number of species per million hectares					Countries
6 MAMMALS	7 BIRDS	8 REPTILES	9 AMPHIBIANS	10 PLANTS	
–	–	–	–	–	Cyprus
41	101	5	10	–	Czech Republic
27	121	3	9	895	Denmark
–	–	–	–	–	Djibouti
12	81	69	21	3,354	Dominican Republic
100	460	126	141	6,421	Ecuador
21	33	18	1	454	Egypt
106	196	57	18	2,277	El Salvador
131	194	–	–	2,312	Equatorial Guinea
50	141	38	8	–	Eritrea
40	130	3	7	1,018	Estonia
54	133	40	13	1,398	Ethiopia
3	61	20	2	1,334	Fiji
19	78	2	2	345	Finland
25	72	9	9	1,233	France
64	157	–	–	2,248	Gabon
112	269	45	29	935	Gambia
56	–	27	7	2,292	Georgia
23	73	4	6	824	Germany
78	186	–	–	1,308	Ghana
41	107	24	6	2,131	Greece
114	208	107	49	3,948	Guatemala
66	142	–	–	1,043	Guinea
71	159	–	–	655	Guinea Bissau
70	246	–	–	2,329	Guyana
2	54	77	40	3,743	Haiti
78	190	73	36	2,559	Honduras
40	98	7	8	1,155	Hungary
5	41	0	0	175	Iceland
47	137	58	31	2,363	India
81	271	91	50	5,196	Indonesia
26	60	31	2	1,489	Iran
23	49	23	2	–	Iraq
13	75	1	2	499	Ireland
91	141	76	5	2,194	Israel
29	76	13	13	1,820	Italy
23	110	35	23	3,207	Jamaica
57	75	26	18	1,679	Japan
34	68	35	–	1,069	Jordan
28	62	8	2	–	Kazakhstan
94	222	50	23	1,703	Kenya
31	–	12	1	1,412	Kirgistan
–	51	8	6	1,274	Korea (North)

PROTECTED ECOSYSTEMS AND BIODIVERSITY

Country	1 LAND AREA 000 hectares	2 TROPICAL FOREST 000 hectares	% protected	3 TEMPERATE FOREST 000 hectares	% protected	4 MANGROVES 000 hectares	% protected	5 WETLANDS 000 hectares protected
Korea (South)	9,873	0	0	1,426	3.4	0	0	1
Kuwait	1,782	–	–	–	–	–	–	–
Laos	23,080	3,639	23	849	5	0	0	–
Latvia	6,205	0	0	1,624	10.1	0	0	43
Lebanon	1,023	0	0	36	0	0	0	1
Lesotho	3,035	89	8.7	0	0	0	0	–
Liberia	9,632	3,149	2.9	0	0	0	0	–
Libya	175,954	0	0	53	0	0	0	0
Lithuania	6,480	0	0	1,509	10.3	0	0	50
Luxembourg	260	0	0	–	–	–	–	0
Macedonia	2,543	0	0	1,091	9.9	0	0	19
Madagascar	58,154	6,940	5.5	0	0	310	0.2	53
Malawi	9,408	3,830	8.5	0	0	0	0	225
Malaysia	32,855	13,007	11.7	0	0	166	6.6	38
Maldives	–	–	–	–	–	–	–	–
Mali	122,019	6,132	2.3	0	0	0	0	162
Marshall Islands	–	–	–	–	–	–	–	–
Mauritania	102,522	–	–	–	–	–	–	1,231
Mauritius	203	–	–	–	–	–	–	0
Mexico	190,869	45,765	4.3	21,293	3.1	531*	0	1,157
Moldova	3,297	0	0	143	5.4	0	0	19
Mongolia	156,650	0	0	2,636	25.2	0	0	631
Morocco	44,630	0	0	1,862	2.6	0	0	14
Mozambique	78,409	20,863	7.5	0	0	565	3.7	–
Namibia	82,329	3,436	10.6	0	0	0	0	630
Nepal	14,300	1,162	18.8	2,660	20.7	0	0	18
Netherlands	3,392	0	0	235	7.4	0	0	327
New Zealand	26,799	0	0	4,212	43.8	0	0	39
Nicaragua	12,140	5,322	24.7	0	0	94	14.8	406
Niger	126,670	27	15.6	0	0	0	0	715
Nigeria	91,077	11,634	7.4	0	0	1,145	0	58
Norway	30,683	0	0	8,139	2	0	0	70
Oman	21,246	–	–	–	–	2*	–	–
Pakistan	77,088	807	0.6	2,083	4.7	73	39.9	284
Panama	7,443	3,744	30.9	0	0	180	2.1	111
Papua New Guinea	45,286	35,791	10.7	0	0	459	23.2	595
Paraguay	39,730	9,290	2.6	2,848	4.9	0	0	775
Peru	128,000	75,636	5.1	0	0	5*	0	6,759
Philippines	29,817	2,402	5.2	0	0	161*	0	68
Poland	30,442	0	0	8,939	12.9	0	0	90
Portugal	9,150	0	0	2,661	5.6	0	0	66
Qatar	1,100	–	–	–	–	–	–	–
Romania	23,034	0	0	8,137	2.5	0	0	665

Sources: Col 1: *World Resources 1998-1999*, Table 11.2; Col 2 & 3: *World Resources 2000-2001*, Table FG.2; Col 4: *World Resources 1998-1999*, Table 11.2 and * *World Resources 2000-2001*, Table CMI.3; Col 5: Wetlands International, August 2002

SPECIES DENSITY Number of species per million hectares					Countries
6 MAMMALS	7 BIRDS	8 REPTILES	9 AMPHIBIANS	10 PLANTS	
23	53	12	7	1,359	Korea (South)
17	17	24	2	193	Kuwait
61	171	23	13	–	Laos
45	117	4	7	651	Latvia
56	152	41	8	2,961	Lebanon
23	40	–	–	1,103	Lesotho
87	168	28	17	993	Liberia
14	17	10	1	331	Libya
37	109	4	7	967	Lithuania
–	–	–	–	–	Luxembourg
57	154	23	10	2,563	Macedonia
37	53	95	47	2,479	Madagascar
86	230	55	31	1,665	Malawi
95	160	110	60	4,890	Malaysia
–	–	–	–	–	Maldives
28	81	3	–	355	Mali
–	–	–	–	–	Marshall Islands
13	59	–	–	239	Mauritania
–	–	–	–	–	Mauritius
86	135	123	54	4,569	Mexico
46	119	6	9	1,173	Moldova
25	80	4	1	533	Mongolia
30	60	26	3	1,049	Morocco
42	117	39	15	1,340	Mozambique
58	109	58	12	942	Namibia
75	252	41	18	2,871	Nepal
35	120	4	10	767	Netherlands
1	51	18	1	802	New Zealand
86	207	69	25	3,256	Nicaragua
27	60	–	–	238	Niger
62	135	30	24	1,059	Nigeria
17	77	2	2	544	Norway
20	39	23	–	439	Oman
36	88	41	4	1,168	Pakistan
112	376	116	84	5,088	Panama
63	184	79	63	3,257	Papua New Guinea
90	164	35	25	2,311	Paraguay
93	310	73	76	3,674	Peru
51	64	62	30	2,907	Philippines
27	72	3	6	778	Poland
30	100	14	8	2,428	Portugal
–	–	–	–	–	Qatar
29	87	9	7	1,194	Romania

Cols 6–8: *World Resources 2000-2001*, Table BI.2; Cols 9–10: *World Resources 2000-2001*, Table BI.3

PROTECTED ECOSYSTEMS AND BIODIVERSITY

Country	1 LAND AREA 000 hectares	2 TROPICAL FOREST 000 hectares	 % protected	3 TEMPERATE FOREST 000 hectares	 % protected	4 MANGROVES 000 hectares	 % protected	5 WETLANDS 000 hectares protected
Russia	1,688,850	0	0	815,551	1.8	0	0	10,324
Rwanda	2,467	291	77	0		0	0	–
Samoa	–	–	–	–	–	–	–	–
Saudi Arabia	214,969	–	–	–	–	29*	–	–
Senegal	19,253	2,076	7	0	0	158	2.9	100
Serbia & Montenegro	10,200	0	0	3,664	3.4	0	0	40
Seychelles	46	–	–	–	–	–	–	–
Sierra Leone	7,162	260	20.3	0	0	176	0.8	295
Singapore	61	–	–	–	–	0.6*	–	–
Slovakia	4,808	0	0	2,308	29.6	0	0	38
Slovenia	2,012	0	0	696	8.9	0	0	1
Solomon Islands	2,799	2,669	0	0	0	64*	0	–
Somalia	62,734	11,800	1.1	0	0	91*	0	–
South Africa	122,104	10,333	5.2	52	26.4	1*	0	499
Spain	49,944	0	0	14,024	10.8	0	0	158
Sri Lanka	6,463	1,581	27.6	0	0	9	9.2	8
Sudan	237,600	12,288	12.3	0	0	94*	0	–
Suriname	15,600	13,219	4	0	0	109	35.9	12
Swaziland	1,720	–	–	–	–	0	0	–
Sweden	41,162	0	0	29,364	1.6	0	0	515
Switzerland	3,955	0	0	1,309	12.6	0	0	8
Syria	18,378	–	–	47	0	–	–	10
Tajikistan	14,060	–	–	–	–	–	–	95
Tanzania	88,359	14,356	15.8	0	0	323	0.4	4,272
Thailand	51,089	16,237	31.2	361	11.3	509	5	132
Togo	5,439	224	2.6	0	0	3*	0	194
Trinidad & Tobago	513	124	7	0	0	5	5.9	6
Tunisia	15,536	0	0	300	2.2	0	0	13
Turkey	76,963	0	0	8,390	1.2	0	0	159
Turkmenistan	46,993	0	0	216	0.7	0	0	–
Uganda	19,965	3,772	17	0	0	0	0	15
Ukraine	57,935	0	0	7,046	1.6	0	0	716
United Arab Emirates	8,360	–	–	–	–	3*	–	–
United Kingdom	24,160	0	0	2,303	20.7	0	0	855
United States of America	915,912	443	6.7	279,386	10.4	199	60	1,190
Uruguay	17,481	2	0	97	1	0	0	407
Uzbekistan	41,424	0	0	231	0	0	0	31
Venezuela	88,205	55,615	59	0	0	621	65.1	264
Vietnam	32,549	4,218	10.3	723	8.8	73	2.2	12
Western Sahara	26,600	–	–	–	–	–	–	–
Yemen	52,797	–	–	–	–	8*	–	–
Zambia	74,339	21,989	31.9	0	0	0	0	333
Zimbabwe	38,685	15,397	12.2	0	0	0	0	

Sources: Col 1: *World Resources 1998-1999*, Table 11.2; Col 2 & 3: *World Resources 2000-2001*, Table FG.2; Col 4: *World Resources 1998-1999*, Table 11.2 and * *World Resources 2000-2001*, Table CMI.3; Col 5: Wetlands International, August 2002

SPECIES DENSITY Number of species per million hectares					Countries
6 MAMMALS	7 BIRDS	8 REPTILES	9 AMPHIBIANS	10 PLANTS	
23	58	5	4	–	Russia
110	373	–	–	1,664	Rwanda
–	–	–	–	–	Samoa
13	26	14	–	345	Saudi Arabia
72	144	37	1	780	Senegal
45	104	33	10	1,896	Serbia & Montenegro
–	–	–	–	–	Seychelles
77	243	–	–	1,091	Sierra Leone
213	295	350	60	5,713	Singapore
50	124	12	12	1,849	Slovakia
59	164	20	16	2,535	Slovenia
37	115	43	12	2,235	Solomon Islands
43	107	49	7	768	Somalia
52	122	65	22	4,797	South Africa
22	76	15	8	1,383	Spain
47	134	77	21	1,781	Sri Lanka
43	110	–	–	507	Sudan
72	240	60	38	1,997	Suriname
–	–	–	–	–	Swaziland
17	71	2	4	498	Sweden
47	121	9	11	1,898	Switzerland
24	78	–	–	1,145	Syria
35	–	18	1	–	Tajikistan
70	184	64	30	2,231	Tanzania
72	168	81	31	3,170	Thailand
110	220	–	–	1,739	Togo
125	324	87	32	2,816	Trinidad & Tobago
31	69	25	3	873	Tunisia
28	72	25	4	2,059	Turkey
29	–	23	1	–	Turkmenistan
118	290	52	17	1,891	Uganda
28	68	5	4	1,318	Ukraine
12	33	18	–	–	United Arab Emirates
17	80	3	2	565	United Kingdom
45	68	30	28	2,036	United States of America
31	92	–	–	882	Uruguay
28	–	18	1	1,369	Uzbekistan
73	302	64	55	4,752	Venezuela
67	168	59	25	3,306	Vietnam
–	–	–	–	–	Western Sahara
18	39	21	–	446	Yemen
56	145	35	16	1,141	Zambia
81	159	46	36	1,325	Zimbabwe

THREATENED SPECIES

Countries	Number of Threatened Species					
	1 PRIMATES	2 BIG CATS	3 UNGULATES	4 RODENTS	5 BATS	6 DOLPHINS AND WHALES
Afghanistan	–	4	4	1	5	–
Albania	–	–	–	–	2	–
Algeria	1	5	7	–	4	–
Angola	4	2	1	2	3	2
Argentina	2	2	6	7	2	5
Armenia	–	–	3	1	2	–
Australia	–	–	1	16	8	5
Austria	–	–	–	2	6	–
Azerbaijan	–	–	4	1	6	–
Bahamas	–	–	–	1	1	1
Bahrain	–	–	–	–	–	–
Bangladesh	4	2	3	3	–	4
Barbados	–	–	–	–	–	–
Belarus	–	–	1	–	1	–
Belgium	–	–	–	1	5	4
Belize	1	–	1	–	1	–
Benin	3	2	1	–	1	–
Bhutan	1	3	6	2	–	1
Bolivia	2	1	2	–	1	–
Bosnia-Herzegovina		–	–	2	7	–
Botswana	–	2	–	–	–	–
Brazil	39	–	1	13	14	4
Brunei	1	3	–	–	–	–
Bulgaria	–	–	–	4	7	2
Burkina Faso	–	2	3	–	–	–
Burma	4	2	9	6	2	3
Burundi	3	2	–	1	–	–
Cambodia	6	2	6	3	–	–
Cameroon	14	2	1	9	2	–
Canada	–	1	1	1	1	8
Cape Verde	–	–	–	–	–	3
Central African Rep.	4	2	1	2	–	–
Chad	–	2	8	1	1	–
Chile	–	2	3	4	3	4
China	11	7	18	16	2	5
Colombia	21	–	2	4	8	2
Comoros	1	–	–	–	–	–
Congo	7	1	1	3	8	1
Congo, Dem. Rep.	9	–	–	–	–	–
Costa Rica	8	–	1	2	2	1
Côte-d'Ivoire	7	1	3	–	3	–
Croatia	–	–	–	1	7	1
Cuba	–	–	–	6	2	

 Source: Data compiled by Richard Mackay from *2000 IUCN Red List of Threatened Species*, IUCN – The World Conservation Union

Number of Threatened Species						Countries
7 REPTILES	8 AMPHIBIANS	9 INVERTEBRATES	10 FISH	11 BIRDS	12 PLANTS	
1	1	1	0	17	4	Afghanistan
4	2	4	17	9	79	Albania
2	1	12	10	11	141	Algeria
4	0	6	9	20	30	Angola
5	30	10	12	55	247	Argentina
5	0	7	1	12	31	Armenia
38	47	283	74	60	2,245	Australia
0	0	44	7	8	23	Austria
5	0	6	5	11	28	Azerbaijan
6	0	1	15	10	31	Bahamas
4	0	0	6	7	–	Bahrain
20	0	0	8	23	24	Bangladesh
4	0	0	11	3	2	Barbados
0	0	8	0	4	1	Belarus
0	0	11	6	10	2	Belgium
4	6	1	18	3	57	Belize
1	0	0	8	2	4	Benin
0	1	1	0	18	23	Bhutan
2	21	1	0	30	227	Bolivia
1	1	10	11	8	64	Bosnia-Herzegovina
0	0	0	0	9	7	Botswana
22	110	34	42	120	1,358	Brazil
4	3	0	6	25	25	Brunei
2	0	9	10	11	106	Bulgaria
1	0	0	0	2	–	Burkina Faso
20	0	2	7	41	32	Burma
0	6	4	0	9	–	Burundi
10	3	0	12	24	5	Cambodia
1	50	4	35	18	89	Cameroon
2	1	11	24	19	278	Canada
0	0	0	14	4	1	Cape Verde
1	0	0	0	3	1	Central African Rep.
1	0	1	0	5	12	Chad
0	20	0	9	32	329	Chile
31	86	4	47	82	312	China
15	208	0	23	86	712	Colombia
2	0	4	4	10	4	Comoros
1	0	1	10	4	3	Congo
2	13	22	10	30	78	Congo, Dem. Rep.
8	60	9	13	18	527	Costa Rica
2	14	1	11	11	94	Côte-d'Ivoire
1	2	11	27	9	6	Croatia
7	47	3	23	18	888	Cuba

115

THREATENED SPECIES

Countries	Number of Threatened Species					
	1 PRIMATES	2 BIG CATS	3 UNGULATES	4 RODENTS	5 BATS	6 DOLPHINS AND WHALES
Cyprus	–	–	2	–	1	–
Czech Republic	–	–	–	2	5	–
Denmark	–	–	–	–	2	–
Djibouti	–	–	4	–	1	–
Dominican Republic		–	–	1	–	1
Ecuador	8	–	3	73	8	4
Egypt	–	3	5	3	4	–
El Salvador	–	–	–	–	2	–
Equatorial Guinea	18	–	–	1	1	–
Eritrea	–	2	4	–	2	1
Estonia	–	–	–	1	1	1
Ethiopia	–	2	11	5	7	–
Fiji	–	–	–	–	4	1
Finland	–	–	–	1	1	3
France	–	–	1	1	8	4
Gabon	9	1	–	1	1	–
Gambia	2	1	1	–	–	–
Georgia	–	–	4	1	6	2
Germany	–	–	–	2	5	4
Ghana	6	1	1	2	2	–
Greece	–	–	1	4	5	–
Guatemala	2	–	–	1	2	–
Guinea	5	1	–	–	2	–
Guinea Bissau	3	1	2	–	–	–
Guyana	–	–	–	1	–	1
Haiti	–	–	–	2	–	–
Honduras	–	–	1	1	2	–
Hungary	–	–	–	2	7	–
Iceland	–	–	–	–	–	6
India	9	5	19	16	10	7
Indonesia	15	6	8	46	32	5
Iran	–	5	3	5	8	–
Iraq	–	2	2	1	4	2
Ireland	–	–	–	–	1	3
Israel	–	2	6	3	5	–
Italy	–	–	2	1	7	2
Jamaica	–	–	–	1	3	–
Japan	2	1	1	5	12	8
Jordan	–	1	3	–	3	–
Kazakhstan	–	3	4	5	4	–
Kenya	2	2	5	11	6	5
Kirgistan	–	3	2	2	1	–
Korea (North)	–	2	2	–	1	–

 Source: Data compiled by Richard Mackay from *2000 IUCN Red List of Threatened Species*, IUCN – The World Conservation Union

Number of Threatened Species						Countries
7 REPTILES	8 AMPHIBIANS	9 INVERTEBRATES	10 FISH	11 BIRDS	12 PLANTS	
3	0	0	7	11	51	Cyprus
0	0	19	7	9	–	Czech Republic
0	0	11	7	10	2	Denmark
0	0	0	9	6	2	Djibouti
10	31	2	10	16	–	Dominican Republic
10	163	48	12	69	824	Ecuador
6	0	1	14	17	82	Egypt
5	8	1	5	3	42	El Salvador
2	5	2	8	6	11	Equatorial Guinea
6	0	0	9	7	–	Eritrea
0	0	4	1	3	2	Estonia
1	9	6	0	20	163	Ethiopia
6	1	2	8	13	74	Fiji
0	0	10	1	10	6	Finland
3	3	65	16	15	195	France
1	2	1	12	5	91	Gabon
1	0	0	11	2	1	Gambia
7	1	10	6	8	29	Georgia
0	0	31	12	14	4	Germany
2	10	0	8	8	103	Ghana
6	4	11	27	14	571	Greece
10	74	8	14	10	355	Guatemala
1	5	3	8	10	39	Guinea
1	0	1	10	1	–	Guinea Bissau
6	6	1	13	3	152	Guyana
9	46	2	12	15	100	Haiti
10	53	2	14	6	96	Honduras
1	0	25	8	9	30	Hungary
0	0	0	8	0	1	Iceland
25	66	23	28	79	1,236	India
28	33	31	91	121	264	Indonesia
8	4	3	14	18	2	Iran
2	1	2	3	18	–	Iraq
0	0	3	6	8	1	Ireland
4	0	10	12	18	32	Israel
4	5	58	17	15	311	Italy
8	17	5	12	12	744	Jamaica
11	20	45	27	53	707	Japan
1	0	3	5	14	9	Jordan
2	1	4	7	23	71	Kazakhstan
5	4	27	29	28	240	Kenya
2	0	3	0	4	34	Kirgistan
0	1	1	5	22	4	Korea (North)

THREATENED SPECIES

Countries	Number of Threatened Species					
	1 PRIMATES	2 BIG CATS	3 UNGULATES	4 RODENTS	5 BATS	6 DOLPHINS AND WHALES
Korea (South)	–	1	2	–	1	–
Kuwait		1	1	–	–	–
Laos	8	2	8	3	–	–
Latvia	–	–	–	1	2	–
Lebanon	–	–	–	–	5	1
Lesotho	–	1	–	–	–	–
Liberia	4	–	3	–	3	1
Libya	–	2	4	3	1	–
Lithuania	–	–	1	1	2	1
Luxembourg	–	–	–	1	5	–
Macedonia	–	–	–	3	7	–
Madagascar	39	–	–	5	7	2
Malawi	–	2	–	1	–	–
Malaysia	6	4	4	8	7	3
Maldives	–	–	–	–	–	–
Mali	2	2	7	1	–	–
Marshall Islands	–	–	–	–	–	1
Mauritania	–	2	5	2	–	1
Mauritius	–	–	–	–	3	–
Mexico	2	2	2	33	14	8
Moldova	–	–	1	1	1	1
Mongolia	–	1	4	3	–	–
Morocco	1	5	4	3	6	2
Mozambique	–	2	–	3	1	3
Namibia	–	2	1	1	2	2
Nepal	1	3	11	4	1	1
Netherlands	–	–	–	1	5	4
New Zealand	–	–	1	–	2	5
Nicaragua	1	–	1	–	1	1
Niger	–	3	7	–	–	–
Nigeria	17	2	3	4	3	–
Norway	–	–	–	–	1	7
Oman	–	–	4	1	3	–
Pakistan	–	4	5	2	4	4
Panama	11	–	1	3	1	3
Papua New Guinea	–	–	–	14	20	–
Paraguay	–	–	2	1	1	–
Peru	15	1	2	6	15	3
Philippines	2	–	5	22	10	–
Poland	–	–	1	3	5	6
Portugal	–	1	–	1	8	4
Qatar	–	–	–	–	–	–
Romania	–	–	1	6	7	2

 Source: Data compiled by Richard Mackay from *2000 IUCN Red List of Threatened Species*, IUCN – The World Conservation Union

Number of Threatened Species						Countries
7 REPTILES	8 AMPHIBIANS	9 INVERTEBRATES	10 FISH	11 BIRDS	12 PLANTS	
0	1	1	7	34	60	Korea (South)
1	0	0	6	12	–	Kuwait
11	4	0	6	21	2	Laos
0	0	8	3	8	–	Latvia
1	0	1	9	10	5	Lebanon
0	0	1	1	7	21	Lesotho
2	4	3	8	11	23	Liberia
3	0	0	9	7	57	Libya
0	0	5	3	4	1	Lithuania
0	0	4	0	3	1	Luxembourg
2	0	5	4	9	–	Macedonia
18	55	32	66	34	306	Madagascar
0	5	11	0	13	61	Malawi
21	45	19	34	40	490	Malaysia
2	0	0	8	2	–	Maldives
1	0	0	1	5	15	Mali
					–	Marshall Islands
2	0	1	11	5	3	Mauritania
5	0	32	7	13	294	Mauritius
21	190	41	106	57	1,593	Mexico
1	0	5	9	8	5	Moldova
0	0	3	1	22	–	Mongolia
2	2	8	11	13	186	Morocco
5	3	5	21	23	89	Mozambique
4	1	1	11	18	75	Namibia
6	3	1	0	31	20	Nepal
0	0	7	7	11	1	Netherlands
12	4	14	16	74	211	New_Zealand
8	10	2	17	8	98	Nicaragua
0	0	1	0	2	–	Niger
2	13	1	12	9	37	Nigeria
0	0	9	7	6	12	Norway
4	0	1	18	14	30	Oman
9	0	0	14	30	14	Pakistan
7	52	2	17	20	1,302	Panama
9	10	12	31	33	92	Papua New Guinea
2	0	0	0	27	129	Paraguay
6	78	2	8	94	906	Peru
8	48	19	49	70	360	Philippines
0	0	15	3	12	27	Poland
1	0	82	20	15	269	Portugal
1	0	0	4	7	–	Qatar
2	0	22	10	13	99	Romania

THREATENED SPECIES

Countries	Number of Threatened Species					
	1 PRIMATES	2 BIG CATS	3 UNGULATES	4 RODENTS	5 BATS	6 DOLPHINS AND WHALES
Russia	–	4	7	7	7	9
Rwanda	7	1	–	3	1	––
Samoa	–	–	–	–	2	–
Saudi Arabia	–	2	3	1	3	–
Senegal	3	2	2	1	2	1
Serbia and Montenegro	–	–	–	3	7	–
Seychelles	–	–	1	–	4	–
Sierra Leone	4	1	3	–	1	–
Singapore	1	2	–	1	1	–
Slovakia	–	–	–	2	6	–
Slovenia	–	–	–	1	7	–
Solomon Islands	–	–	–	5	14	1
Somalia	–	2	8	2	1	–
South Africa	–	2	1	5	5	5
Spain	–	1	1	1	9	6
Sri Lanka	2	1	–	3	–	4
Sudan	2	2	11	4	4	–
Suriname	–	–	–	1	3	3
Swaziland	–	2	–	1	–	–
Sweden	–	–	–	–	3	3
Switzerland	–	–	–	1	5	–
Syria	–	2	2	1	1	–
Tajikistan	–	3	3	1	1	–
Tanzania	5	2	4	5	4	5
Thailand	4	3	8	5	4	2
Togo	3	2	2	1	–	–
Trinidad & Tobago	2	–	–	–	–	–
Tunisia	–	4	6	–	4	2
Turkey	–	3	2	4	7	2
Turkmenistan	–	3	5	3	3	–
Uganda	7	2	–	5	1	–
Ukraine	–	–	1	7	6	2
United Arab Emirates	–	1	1	–	–	1
United Kingdom	–	1	1	–	3	8
United States of America	–	4	3	10	6	9
Uruguay	–	–	–	–	1	3
Uzbekistan	–	3	3	2	2	–
Venezuela	4	–	2	5	6	3
Vietnam	11	2	8	5	3	–
Western Sahara	–	3	4	–	–	–
Yemen	–	2	3	–	1	–
Zambia	–	2	–	1	3	–
Zimbabwe	–	2	–	2	4	

 Sources: Cols 1–6, 12: data compiled by Richard Mackay from *2000 IUCN Red List of Threatened Species*, IUCN – The World Conservation Union <www.redlist.org/>;
cols 7–11: <www.redlist.org> summary statistics

Number of Threatened Species						Countries
7 REPTILES	8 AMPHIBIANS	9 INVERTEBRATES	10 FISH	11 BIRDS	12 PLANTS	
6	0	30	18	47	214	Russia
0	8	4	0	9	–	Rwanda
1	0	1	4	7	18	Samoa
2	0	1	9	17	7	Saudi Arabia
6	0	0	18	5	31	Senegal
1	1	19	20	10	155	Serbia & Montenegro
3	6	4	10	13	78	Seychelles
3	2	4	8	10	29	Sierra Leone
4	0	1	13	10	29	Singapore
1	0	19	8	11	–	Slovakia
0	2	42	16	7	13	Slovenia
4	2	6	5	21	42	Solomon Islands
2	0	1	16	13	103	Somalia
20	21	127	49	36	2,215	South Africa
8	4	63	24	20	985	Spain
8	44	2	23	16	455	Sri Lanka
2	0	2	8	10	10	Sudan
6	2	0	12	0	103	Suriname
0	0	0	0	6	42	Swaziland
0	0	13	6	9	13	Sweden
0	1	30	4	8	30	Switzerland
3	0	3	9	11	8	Syria
1	0	2	3	9	50	Tajikistan
5	40	33	28	37	436	Tanzania
19	3	1	36	42	385	Thailand
2	3	0	8	2	4	Togo
5	9	0	15	2	21	Trinidad & Tobago
3	0	5	9	9	24	Tunisia
12	5	13	30	14	1,870	Turkey
2	0	5	8	13	17	Turkmenistan
0	6	19	27	15	15	Uganda
2	0	14	11	13	52	Ukraine
1	0	0	6	11	–	United Arab Emirates
0	0	10	12	10	18	United Kingdom
27	50	561	154	71	4,669	United States of America
3	4	1	11	24	15	Uruguay
2	0	1	4	16	41	Uzbekistan
13	68	1	19	25	46	Venezuela
24	15	0	23	41	341	Vietnam
0	0	1	11	3	–	Western Sahara
2	1	2	11	14	149	Yemen
0	1	7	0	12	12	Zambia
0	6	2	0	10	100	Zimbabwe

REFERENCES

Part 1 EXTINCTION IS FOREVER

12–13 EVOLUTION

C Darwin, *On the Origin of Species by Means of Natural Selection, or The Preservation of Favoured Races in the Struggle for Life*, 1859
<daphne.palomar.edu>
<www.ucmp.berkeley.edu/history/evolution.html>
<www.geocities.com/RainForest/Canopy/3220/taxonomy.html>

14–15 MASS EXTINCTIONS

<www.bbc.co.uk/education/darwin/exfiles/index.htm
<www.wri.org/biodiv/extinct.html>

16–17 HOMINIDS

Institute of Human Origins: <www.asu.edu/clas/iho/>
<www.talkorigins.org>

18–19 HUMAN ENVIRONMENTAL IMPACT

National Geographic, September 2004
Examples of early warning signs of global warming cited on <www.climatehotmap.org>
Global Footprint Network <www.footprintnetwork.org>

Part 2 ECOSYSTEMS

22–23 TROPICAL FORESTS

Food and Agricultural Organization, *State of the World's Forests 1999*, FAO 1999
World Wide Fund for Nature, *Forests for Life*, WWF-UK 1996
Protected Tropical Forest and **Tropical Forest by Region**: *World Resources 2000–2001*, WRI 2000, Table FG.2
Tropical Forest Past and Future: D Bryant, D Nielsen, L Tangley, *The Last Frontier Forests: Ecosystems and Economics on the Edge*, WRI, 1997

24–25 TEMPERATE FORESTS

Food and Agricultural Organization, *State of the World's Forests 1999*, FAO 1999
WWF, *Forests for Life*, WWF-UK 1996
Protected Temperate Forest and **Temperate Forest by Region**: *World Resources 2000–2001*, WRI 2000, Table FG.2
Temperate Forest Past and Future: D Bryant, D Nielsen, L Tangley, *The Last Frontier Forests: Ecosystems and Economics on the Edge*, WRI, 1997

26–27 GRASSLANDS

World Resources 2000–2001, World Resources Institute, 2000 pp119–139
Sauer, J R, J E Hines, I Thomas, J Fallon, and G Gough, *The North American Breeding Bird Survey,*
Results and Analysis 1966–1998. Version 98.1, USGS Patuxent Wildlife Research Center, 1999
Asian steppes: *World Resources 2000-2001,* pp212–224
Grasslands: R White, S Murray, M Rohweder, PAGE Analysis, Map 15
<www.wri.org/wr2000/grasslands_page.html>
Current Land Use: *World Resources 2000-2001*, p123

28–29 WETLANDS

Wetlands International <www.ramsar.org>
International Rivers Network <www.irn.org>
WWF <www.panda.org>
Wetlands of International Importance: *Ramsar Sites: Directory and Overview. A guide to the Ramsar Convention's Wetlands of International Importance* Wetlands International, August 2002
Florida Mangroves: <www.unep-wcmc.org>
Mangrove loss in Thailand: <www.agri-aqua.ait.ac.th/mangroves/Costtab3.html>

30–31 CORAL REEFS

D Bryant, L Burke, J McManus, M Spalding, *Reefs at Risk*, World Resources Institute, 1998
The State of Coral: World Conservation Monitoring Centre, 1997 <www.unep-wcmc.org>
Coral Reef Destroyed: C Wilkinson, *Status of Coral Reefs of the World: 2000*, Australian Institute of Marine Science, 2000

32–33 OCEANS

A Freiwald, JH Fosså, A Grehan, T Koslow, JM Roberts, 2004. *Cold-water Coral Reefs*. UNEP-WCMC, Cambridge, UK
M Giannia, 2004. *High Seas Bottom Trawl Fisheries and their Impacts on the Biodiversity of Vulnerable Deep-Sea Ecosystems: Options for International Action*. IUCN – The World Conservation Union
Lack, M., Short, K. and Willock, A. (2003). *Managing risk and uncertainty in deep-sea fisheries: lessons from Orange Roughy*. TRAFFIC Oceania and WWF Australia.
World Energy Council (2001). *Survey of Energy Resources*. <www.worldenergy.org/wec-geis/publications/reports/ser/overview.asp>
WWF briefing, at: <www.ngo.grida.no/wwfneap/Publication/briefings/LuckyStrike.pdf>
Joint Nature Conservation Committee statement at: <www.jncc.gov.uk/page-1449>
Deep-sea Bed Polymetallic Nodule Exploration: Development of Environmental Guidelines. Proceedings of the International Seabed Authority's Workshop held in Sanya, Hainan Island, People's Republic of China, 1-5 June 1998 (ISA/99/02)

International Seabed Authority, *Marine Mineral Resources*, factsheet <www.isa.org.jm/en/ seabedarea/TechBrochures/ENG6.pdf>

<www.greenpeace.org.au/oceans/save_deep_sea_life/c reatures_of_the_seamounts.html>

Ray Boswell, 'Buried Treasure' The American Association of Mechanical Engineers February 2005 <www.memagazine.org>

Hans Greimel, 'Resource-poor Japan is banking on ice that burns as future fuel source' July 3, 2003 <www.climateark.org>

Part 3 FRAGILE REGIONS
36–37 THE ARCTIC
C Zöckler & I Lysenko, *Water Birds on the Edge* (March 2000) World Conservation Monitoring Centre

Protected Areas: Conservation of Arctic Flora and Fauna <www.grida.no.db/maps/caff>

Red-Breasted Goose: J M Hunter & J M Black, *International Action Plan for the Red-Breasted Goose*, BirdLife International, European Commission <europa.eu.int/comm/environment/nature/directive/ birdactionplan/brantaruficollis.htm>

38–39 THE ANTARCTIC
The World Factbook, 2000, Central Intelligence Agency, 2000

2000 IUCN Red List of Threatened Species, IUCN – The WorldConservation Union

Protected Areas: <www.nerc-bas.ac.uk/ public/magic/protected-area/spa/spamap.html>

Southern Ocean Sanctuary: <ourworld.compuserve. com/homepages/iwcoffice/Catches.htm>

National Geographic, September 2004

Larsen B Ice-Shelf Collapses, March 21, 2002 <nsidc.org>

Antarctic warming killing off fish food, Patricia Reaney, November 4, 2004 <abc.net.au>

40–41 AUSTRALIA
National Geographic, insert on Australia, Washington, July 2000

World Heritage Sites: <www.unesco.org/whc>

Threatened Species and **Degree of Threat:** IUCN Red List 2000

42–43 CENTRAL AND SOUTH AMERICA
John Vidal, 'Road to Oblivion' *Guardian*, June 11, 2001, G2, p6, quoting William Laurence of Smithsonian Institute in *Science*, January 19, 2001

Monitoring of the Brazilian Amazonian Forest by Satellite 1998 to 1999, Instituto Nacional de Pesquisas Espaciais, April 2000

Protected Land: *World Resources 2000–2001*, WRI, 2000, Table BI.1

World Heritage Sites: <www.unesco.org/whc/nwhc/pages/sites/main.htm>

Amazon Basin: <www.unep-wcmc.org>

44–45 GALAPAGOS
Galapagos Conservation Trust <www.gct.org>

Galapagos Coalition <serv1.law.emory.edu/sites/GALAPAGOS/>

Darwin Foundation <www.darwinfoundation.org>

<www.wwf.org/galapagos/iguana.htm> <www.geocities. com/RainForest/Jungle/7751/lavagull.html>

46–47 MADAGASCAR
Protected Areas: <www.wcmc.org.uk/cgi-bin/pa_paisquery.p>

Threatened Animals, Degree of Threat, Threatened Plant Species: <www.redlist.org>

Madagascar Rosy Periwinkle: <www.mobot.org>

<www.panda.org> <www.lib.utexas.edu>

<www.chass.utoronto.ca/anthropology>

Part 4 ENDANGERED ANIMALS AND PLANTS
50–51 PRIMATES
P Day, "British Biologist Warns of Threat to Monkeys", *Daily Telegraph*, October 31, 1999, p16

Duke University Primate Center <www.duke.edu/web/primate>

G Lean & D Hinrichsen *Atlas of the Environment*, Helicon 1992

University of Manitoba <www.umanitoba.ca> <www.columbia.edu/cu/pr/96_99/19244.html> <www.panda.org>

Threatened Primates: *2000 IUCN Red List of Threatened Species* <www.redlist.org/>

52–53 BIG CATS
<web.inter.nl.net/users/tiger/aboutset.html>

<www.snowleopard.org/facts.html>

<www.halcyon.com/mongolia/snowleopard.html>

Threatened Big Cats: *2000 IUCN Red List of Threatened Species*, <www.redlist.org>

Decline of the Tiger: Zoe Foundation

54–55 UNGULATES
Threatened Ungulates: *2000 IUCN Red List of Threatened Species*, <www.redlist.org>

Changing Fortunes of the North American Bison: <bisoncentral.com>

Wild Population of Arabian Oryx: <www.animalinfo.org/index.htm>

Baby pygmy hog: Durrell Wildlife Conservation Trust <www.durrellwildlife.org>

56–57 ELEPHANTS & RHINOS

Distribution of Elephants and Rhinos: *2000 IUCN Red List of Threatened Species* <www.redlist.org> International Rhino Foundation <www.rhinos-irf.org>

58–59 BEARS

Elizabeth Kemf, Alison Wilson and Christopher Servheen, *Bears in the Wild*, WWF, 1999

Threatened Bears and **Threatened Pandas:** *2000 IUCN Red List of Threatened Species* <www.redlist.org>

Population of Threatened Bears: <www.panda.org>

Brown bear: Hunters kill last female bear native to Pyrenees, November 4, 2004 <www.timesonline.co.uk>

Giant pandas: Hungry giant pandas to get new food source, *China Daily*, March 28, 2005

60–61 RODENTS

Ronald Nowak, *Walker's Mammals of the World*, 6th Edition, Vol II. Baltimore and London: The Johns Hopkins University Press, 1999

Threatened Rodents: *2000 IUCN Red List of Threatened Species* <www.redlist.org>

A Marmot on the Brink: A Bryant, *Forestry and historical population dynamics of the endangered Vancouver Island marmot*, Contributed talk, American Society of Mammalogists meeting, Durham, New Hampshire, June 2000 (courtesy of Marmot Recovery Foundation) <www.speciesatrisk.gc.ca>

62–63 BATS

Threatened Bats: *2000 IUCN Red List of Threatened Species*, IUCN – The WorldConservation Union, <www.redlist.org>

64–65 DOLPHINS AND WHALES

Threatened Dolphins and Whales: *2000 IUCN Red List of Threatened Species*, <www.redlist.org>

Great Whale Populations: International Whaling Commission <ourworld.compuserve.com /homepages/iwcoffice/Estimate.htm>

66–67 REPTILES AND AMPHIBIANS

Threatened Reptiles and **Threatened Amphibians:** *2004 IUCN Red List of Threatened Species*, <www.redlist.org>

Disasters take their toll on amphibians <www.climateark.org>

Global Amphibian Assessment <www.globalamphibians.org/index.html>

68–69 INVERTEBRATES

Threatened Invertebrates and **Threatened Crustaceans:** *2004 IUCN Red List of Threatened Species* <www.redlist.org>

Monarch butterfly: Karen Oberhauser and A. Townsend Peterson. *Modeling current and future potential wintering distributions of eastern North American monarch butterflies*. Proceedings of the National Academy of Sciences of the United States of America, 2003 100: 14063-14068

Ladybird: Hunt for the Harlequin – a UK survey for the world's most invasive ladybird. Natural Environment Research Council, press release 15 March 2005. <www.nerc.ac.uk>

70–71 FISH

The State of World Fisheries and Aquaculture 2000, Food and Agriculture Organization Fisheries Department <www.fao.org/fi/default.asp>

Threatened Fish: *2004 IUCN Red List of Threatened Species* <www.redlist.org>

Increase in Fish Catch and **Global Catch:** FAO, 2001 <www.fao.org/fi/default.asp>

72–73 PLANTS

Threatened Plants and **Extent of Threat:** *1997 IUCN Red List of Threatened Plants* <www.redlist.org>

Part 5 Endangered Birds

76–77 BIRDS

Threatened Birds: *2004 IUCN Red List of Threatened Species* <www.redlist.org>

Bird species density: *World Resources 2000-2001*, Table BI.2

Farmland Birds: UK Farmland Bird Population Change: Royal Society for the Protection of Birds <www.rspb.org.uk>

78–79 BIRDS OF PREY

Threatened Birds of Prey: *2000 IUCN Red List of Threatened Species* <www.redlist.org>

Californian Condor in Crisis: US Fish & Wildlife Service, 1996, *Recovery Plan for the California Condor*

Decline of Asian White-backed Vulture: V Prakash, Bombay Natural History Society, quoted on: <www.peregrinefund.org/conserv_vulture.html>

Sanjida O'Connell 'Change in the pecking order' *The Guardian*, October 24, 2002 <www.guardian.co.uk>

RSPB <www.rspb.org.uk/international/vultures/ diclofenac.asp>

Great Philippine eagle: <www.panda.org>

80–81 PARROTS AND COCKATOOS

N Snyder, P McGowan, J Gilardi and A Grajal, eds., 2000, *Parrots: Status Survey and Conservation Action Plan.* Species Survival Commission WWF <www.panda.org>

Threatened Parrots and Cockatoos: *2000 IUCN Red List of Threatened Species* <www.redlist.org>

Puerto Rican Amazon Parrot: C F Quist *et al*, *Granular cell tumor in an endangered Puerto Rican amazon parrot* <www.vet.uga.edu/IVCVM/ 1998/quist/quist.htm>

Yellow-eared Conure: <www.abcbirds.org/
counterparts/project_yellow-eared_parrot.htm>

82–83 SEABIRDS

United Nations General Assembly Resolution 46-215,
December 20, 1991

BirdLife International Seabird Conservation Programme:
<www.uct.ac.za/depts/stats/adu/seabirds/>
<www.baheera.com/inthewild/vanishing.htm>

WWF <www.panda.org>

Threatened Seabirds: *2000 IUCN Red List of
Threatened Species* <www.redlist.org/>

Spectacled petrel: <www.uct.ac.za/depts/stats/adu
/seabirds/wbw/redbook.htm>

Short-tailed albatross: <www.uct.ac.za/depts/stats
/adu/seabirds/>; personal communication from
Hiroshi Hasegawa July 2001

84–85 MIGRATING BIRDS

<www.environment.gov.au/water/wetlands>
<www.panda.org/resources/publications/climate/migr
ation/page5.htm>
<www.ramsar.org/key_montreux_record.htm>

Americas:

<north.audubon.org> <birds.cornell.edu/bow/ruthum/>
<www.ecst.csuchico.edu/~tgeier/bird/pac.html>
<www.ankn.uaf.edu/units/birdslesson5.html>
<www.r5.fs.fed.us/hawk/html/fs_programs.htm>
<arnica.csustan.edu/esrpp/swainson.htm>
<www.panda.org>

Europe and Africa:

International Animal Rescue, Malta
<www.iar.org.uk/malta/index.shtml> 2004

Royal Society for the Protection of Birds
<www.rspb.org.uk/international/illegal_hunting/malt
a/index.asp> April 2004

<orn-lab.ekol.lu.se/birdmigration/migrpatterns>
<www.birdwatchireland.ie>
Guardian Education March 28, 2000
<www.birds.org.il>
<www.terrestrialmap.org/TernWkrm.htm>
<www.wildwatch.com/backissues/feb2001/regulars/
birds.htm>
<www.environment.gov.au/water/wetlands>
<www.zpok.hu/cyanide/baiamare/docs/donana.htm>
<marathonandmore.tripod.com/ornimalta-tourism.html>
<www.unesco.org/whc/nwhc/pages/sites/main.htm>

Asia and Oceania:

<www.environment.gov.au/water/wetlands>
<www.me.go.kr/english/sub/na_3.htm>
<www.tasweb.com.au/awsg/flyways.htm>
<www.environment.gov.au/water/wetlands/mwp/apstr
at.htm#2.1thegeographicregion>
<www.wing-wbsj.or.jp/birdlife/asia_book/news_release.htm>

<www.sanctuaryasia.com/past_articles17.html>

Part 6 ISSUES OF CONSERVATION

88–89 ANIMAL BIODIVERSITY

B Groombridge and M D Jenkins, *Global Biodiversity*,
World Conservation Press, 2000

Animal Biodiversity and **Total Known Species**:
World Resources 2000-2001 WRI, 2000, Table BI.3

90–91 PLANT BIODIVERSITY

B Groombridge and M D Jenkins, *Global Biodiversity*,
World Conservation Press, 2000

Plant Biodiveristy: *World Resources 2000-2001*
Table BI.3

Number of Plant Species: UNEP-WCMC

92–93 ECOLOGICAL HOTSPOTS

Conservation Focus: Conservation International
<www.conservation.org/Hotspots/>; WWF
<www.worldwildlife.org/global200/>
<www.nationalgeographic.com/wildworld/global.htm>

94–95 CONSERVING ANIMALS

Conservation Zoos: <www.cbsg.org>
<www.goodzoos.com/conserva.htm>

Amur leopard: <amur-leopard.org>

Fall and Rise of the Nene: <www.wwt.org.uk>

Durrell Wildlife Conservation Trust:
<www.durrellwildlife.org>

96–97 CONSERVING PLANTS

<www.nps.gov/plants/index.htm>

Plant Research Centers: <www.nybg.org/bsci/ih/>

Kew Gardens: <www.rbgkew.org.uk>

Golden Pagoda: <www.redlist.org>

98–99 CONSERVING DOMESTIC BREEDS

<www.new-agri.co.uk/01-1/focuson/focuson3.html>

Threatened Domestic Breeds: FAO, *World Watch
Lists for Domestic Animal Diversity*, FAO 2000

100–101 IMPORT TRADE

<www. cites.org>

Major Importers: *World Resources 2000–2001*, WRI,
2000 Table BI.4

Rhino horn:
<www.iss.co.za/pubs/asr/6.1/du%20bois.html>

Orang-utan: A Cronin, *Ape Rescue Chronicle*
Summer 2000, <www.monkeyworld.org>

102–103 EXPORT TRADE

Major Exporters: *World Resources 2000–2001*, WRI,
2000 Table BI.4

Sturgeon ban: <www.cites.org/eng/newsl>

Ivory: <www. cites.org>

INDEX